A SERIES OF LESSONS IN ISLAM

Social Affairs

BROTHERHOOD. MARRIAGE. COMMUNITY.

Sayyid Ali Al-Hakeem

THE MAINSTAY
FOUNDATION

Author: Sayyid Ali Al-Hakeem

Translated and Edited by: The Mainstay Foundation

© 2017 The Mainstay Foundation

Printed in the United States.

ISBN: 978-1943393978

To our guide. To our hope. To our salvation.

To our Prophet (s).

CONTENTS

ABOUT THE AUTHOR

Sayyid Ali Al-Hakeem is an esteemed Muslim scholar, lecturer, and researcher residing in Dubai, UAE. Sayyid Al-Hakeem spent ten years studying at the Islamic seminaries of Qum, Iran. There, he completed his Advanced Seminars (a Ph.D. equivalent in Islamic seminaries) in Islamic Jurisprudence and Thought. He also received a Master's degree in Islamic Thought from the Islamic University of Lebanon. Sayyid Al-Hakeem has dedicated the past twenty-two years of his life to service of the Muslim community in different capacities. He serves as a resident scholar in the Imam Hassan Mosque, Dubai. He is the Chair of the Religious Committee and the religious supervisor of the Charitable Deeds Committee of the Ja'afariya Endowment Charitable Council of Dubai.

TRANSLATOR'S PREFACE

The task of translating Sayyid Ali Al-Hakeem's book was gratifying and enlightening. The book delivered precious nuggets of knowledge and polished pearls of wisdom in a style that is conversational and pleasant. This book is our attempt to pass these nuggets and pearls on to you in a style that is similarly conversational and pleasant. We thank the Sayyid for allowing us to benefit from this endeavor. We wish for him a life filled with scholarly attainment, in hopes that he will continue to pass along his treasures.

Here, we must humbly admit some of our biggest limitations. First, we must admit the great difficulty that comes with the attempting to translate the Holy Quran. Muslim scholars have pondered on the meanings of the holy text for centuries, and the meanings of its verses only grow deeper as time passes. The process of translation always begs us to find precise meanings for the passages that we translate. But when we encounter the majesty of the Holy Quran, we find ourselves incapable of understanding, let alone translating, its true and deep meanings. We turned to the works of translators who have attempted to do this before. Although no translation can do justice to the Holy Quran, we found that the translation of Ali Quli Qarai to be the most proper in understanding when compared to the understanding of the text as derived by our grand scholars. As such, we decided to rely on Qarai's translations throughout this book, with some adaptations that allowed us to weave the verses more properly with the rest of the work.

A second great limitation came with translation of the narrations of the Grand Prophet Muhammad (s) and his Holy Household. Their words are ever so deep and ever so powerful. We attempted to convey these passages to the reader in a tone that is understandable without deviating from the essence of the words of these immaculate personalities. We pray that we were successful in this endeavor.

Finally, we want to take this opportunity to thank you for your support. As students of Islam and as translators of this text, our greatest purpose is to please God by passing along these teachings to others. By picking up this book, you've lent your crucial support in this endeavor. We hope that you will continue your support throughout the rest of this book, and we ask that you keep us in prayers whenever you pick it up.

The Editorial and Translation Team,

The Mainstay Foundation

INTRODUCTION

In the name of God the Beneficent the Merciful

Praise be to God, Lord of the Worlds. May God send His peace and blessings to the most noble of His creatures, the Holy Prophet Muhammad (s) and his Holy Progeny (a).

This book, *Social Affairs: Brotherhood, Marriage, Community,* is a compilation of inspirational lessons in regards to living as part of a community. It lays a framework for Islamic teachings on how to be part of the human family. Whether it is a parent, a sibling, a close family member, a fellow mosque goer, a coworker, or an absolute stranger, our faith teaches us how to interact with integrity and respect. The book details the rights and etiquettes taught to us by our Holy Prophet Muhammad (s) and the Immaculate Imams (a) in regards to any individual we may encounter in our lives.

The teachings of Islam have one unequivocal goal – to allow its followers to pursue excellence. From that perspective, Islam places great emphasis on knowledge and learning. We can see this clearly in the verses of the Holy Quran. These verses give knowledge a special status that is unique when compared with other human virtues. God says in the

Holy Quran, "*Say, 'Are those who know equal to those who do not know?' Only those who possess intellect take admonition.*"[1] God also says, "*Only those of God's servants having knowledge fear Him.*"[2]

The traditions of the Holy Prophet (s) and his Progeny (a) contain numerous similar admonitions as well. It is narrated that Imam Al-Sadiq (a) said, "*The Messenger of God (s) once said, 'Seeking knowledge is an obligation on every Muslim. Verily, God loves the seekers of knowledge.*" It is also narrated that the Commander of the Faithful Ali ibn Abi Talib (a) once said,

> *Oh people! Know that excellence in faith consists of seeking knowledge and acting in accordance to that knowledge. Indeed, seeking knowledge is a higher obligation for you than seeking sustenance. Your sustenance is pre-ordained and guaranteed. Your Just Lord has divided it amongst you and promised to deliver it to you. Surely, He will keep His promise. [On the other hand,] knowledge is protected by its keepers. You were commanded to seek it from its keepers, so go forth and seek it.*

Islam did not stop at admonitions and theories about knowledge and learning. Instead, it created opportunities and enabled conditions that would foster learning, research, and study. Amongst these was the establishment of Friday prayers – God says in the Quran, "*O you who have faith! When the call is made for prayer on Friday, hurry toward the remembrance of God, and leave all business. That is better for you, should you know.*"[3] One of the important pillars of this ritual is its sermon, where the prayer leader must convey Islam's teachings, in

---

[1] The Holy Quran. Chapter 39 [Arabic: *Al-Zumar*]. Verse 9.
[2] The Holy Quran. Chapter 35 [Arabic: *Fatir*]. Verse 28.
[3] The Holy Quran. Chapter 62 [Friday; Arabic: *Al-Jum'a*]. Verse 9.

addition to addressing all other relevant worldly and other-worldly matters.

Dear reader, this series of books is based on a compilation of Friday sermons that I delivered over the years, as well as lectures I gave at a number of commemorations and celebrations. Throughout such gatherings, I have been able to address and speak on a wide array of issues relevant to the Muslim community.

At the insistence of a number of dear brothers, I compiled my notes to write these books with the hopes that God will accept the work and that the benefit will spread to the believers. I tried to maintain the conversational tone of the original sermons in order to make the books more reader friendly. After a series of these books were printed in the original Arabic, a group of believers then insisted to have the work translated into English so that English-speaking audiences may benefit as well.

I thank God, the Exalted, for His infinite support and favor. I must also thank everyone who participated in making this book a reality.

I ask God, the Almighty, to take this work as an act of devotion for His sake and to accept it by His grace, He is surely the All-Kind and Magnanimous.

Ali Al-Hakeem,

Dubai, United Arab Emirates

THE HUMAN FAMILY

In the name of God, the most Beneficent, the most Merciful

The believers are but brethren, therefore make peace between your brethren and be careful of [your duty to] God so that mercy may be had on you.[1]

As human beings we long for bonding with our fellow human beings. It is part of our nature to live and coexist with one another. Building relationships of mutual benefit is part and parcel to human tradition. We cannot exist without one another. From the institution of marriage and raising a family to engaging in trade and general socialization, we yearn for these relationships. Isolation is not natural to the human condition. It is rarely chosen out of free will and is often only imposed by necessity or circumstance. Islam embraces the nature of man and encourages his integration with the rest of mankind. Society is built upon individual engagement forming the collective of families, groups, and communities. Islam empowers individuals to acknowledge each other, in all their diversity, appreciate one another and learn

---

[1] The Holy Quran. Chapter 49. [The Inner Apartments; Arabic: *Al-Hujraat*]. Verse 10.

5

more about that diversity that exists amongst them. Out of this great family we call mankind, we find this diversity and celebrate it.

God says in the Holy Quran,

> O you men, surely We have created you of a male and a female, and made you tribes and families that you may know each other; surely the most honorable of you with God is the one among you most careful [of his duty]; surely God is Knowing, Aware.[2]

Identifying people into nations and tribes is for the fundamental purpose of learning and engagement. We are all different as we come from diverse experiences, backgrounds, traditions and customs. God created us this way in order that we appreciate those differences and learn from one another. The traditions of Ahlulbayt reiterate this notion and emphasize that a person cannot do without others.

Marazem, one of the companions of Imam Al-Sadiq, narrates that he said, "A person cannot do without others in his life... People are in need of one another."[3]

In light of this, we find it quite important to study and discuss subjects within the domain of the great human family. Topics in brotherhood, family, marriage, community, and other aspects of social relations are vital to our understanding of one another and our ethics. We can deepen our understanding of Islam's philosophy on these pertinent social topics, like brotherhood and marriage, by looking at the tra-

---

[2] The Holy Quran. Chapter 49 [The Inner Apartments; Arabic: *Al-Hujraat*]. Verse 13.

[3] Al-Kulayni, *Al-Kafi*, 2:635.

ditions of Ahlulbayt pertaining to community engagement, mainly being isolation and integration. Equally important is studying the foundations for the concept of brotherhood between the believers.

ISOLATION AND INTEGRATION

There are generally two approaches to community engagement found in the text of the narrations from the Holy Prophet and his household. The first approach is to isolate oneself from his community, not associate with others, and avoid engaging with people. The purpose behind this approach is essentially to abstain from committing sins and avert delving into problems with others.

Hafath Ibn Ghiyath narrates that Imam Al-Sadiq said,

> *If you are able to not leave your home, do so. If you do leave your home, you should not backbite, lie, envy, show hypocrisy, be fake, or cajole… A person's home is his sanctuary; in it he protects his sight, tongue, soul, and private parts.*[4]

In another narration from Hisham Ibn Al-Hakam he says that Imam Al-Kadhim expressed a similar sentiment regarding solitude.

> *O Hisham, being patient with being alone is a sign of the strength of the intellect… Surely, whoever attains understanding of God [and His commands] will abandon the people of this world and those who desire it and seek that which is with God… God is his pleasure in his solitude and his friend when he is alone, and He will suffice him in*

---

[4] Ibid.

*his time of need and God is his honor when he has no fami-
ly.*[5]

The second approach is much different than the first. This
of narrations encourage people to integrate and engage with
others, while implicitly condemning isolation. In fact, some
narrations condemn isolation outright and look down upon
those who do not take their fellow man as brethren or
friend.

One of the companions of Imam Al-Sadiq was speaking to
him about a member of the community that chose isolation
instead of integration. He said, "May I be sacrificed for
you... he remained in his home and did not get to know any
of his brothers." The Imam replied, "Then, how does this
man learn his faith?"[6] Essentially, if he is not engaging with
his brothers in faith then how is it practicing that very faith.

Marazem narrates another tradition from Imam Al-Sadiq
where he says,

> *Unto you is performing prayers in the mosque, being good
> neighbors to others, providing testimony, and attending fu-
> nerals. You have no alternative to associating with people,
> for one cannot do without others in his life. You need one
> another.*[7]

There are plenty of other traditions, like these, that highlight
the importance of engaging and connecting with people.
Our scholars have attempted to reconcile between these
two seemingly contradicting types of traditions. When we

---

[5] Ibid.

[6] ibid.

[7] Ibid.

look deeper, however, they are not in contradiction but merely apply exceptions with secondary circumstances. The majority of scholars agree that God has generally called for people to engage and associate with one another, and to cultivate effective meaningful social relationships. The traditions that refer to isolation are only applicable to specific situations. In essence, they are the exception to the rule.

To further explain this, we will touch on some of the scholarly opinions that show the preference for association over isolation, and define precisely what is intended by isolation.

First, there is no doubt that associating with others will render righteous deeds, such as visiting the ill, participating in funerals, fulfilling the needs of believers, extending a hand to the poor, and commemorating the Holy Household.

Isolation deprives one from these virtuous acts. The traditions that are relayed about isolation are intended to protect against people's evils. They advise one to distance himself from others if the association will render bad deeds and detriment one's faith. Otherwise, associating with the righteous and guiding the misguided is the path of the Prophets and the best of worship.[8]

Second, the desirable isolation is that of the heart. The great scholar Al-Majlisi describes isolation as,

> *Seclusion of the heart from the evil acts of people and not depending on them and relying on God alone. It is benefiting from the good of people and being precautious of their misdeeds.[9]*

[8] Al-Majlisi, 'Ain Al-Hayat, 1:352.
[9] Ibid.

Perhaps some of the traditions on isolation are suggesting the benefits of isolation within this meaning or understanding. Take for example the narration by Safwan Al-Jamal from Imam Al-Sadiq where he said,

> *Blessed is a little-known servant who knew people and befriended them with his body, and did not associate with them in their actions with his heart; thus, he knew them from the outside and they did not know him from the inside.*[10]

Third, the traditions that preach for isolation can be interpreted as the author of *Al-Wasa'el* interpreted them in his commentary on such traditions. He analyzed that they are specific to exceptional situations where a person finds himself weak before societal pressure and temptation. Thus, he would take precaution with isolation as his only viable measure to avert the ill doings produced from his association with others. Alternatively, it can also be interpreted as a way to educate and warn about the downsides of association, as it is something that is necessary and indispensable in one's life.[11]

Fourth, a person's purpose on this earth is to be tried and tested. God created mankind to be tested and tried and reach perfection. He is to choose the truth as opposed to falsehood and the righteous as opposed to the corrupt. All of this is in line with his natural course in the universe and

---

[10] Al-Sadouq, *Al-Khisal*, 28.

[11] Al-Hakeem, *Al-Jama'a Al-Saliha*, 1:47.

society, and evading the trials and tribulations by avoiding society does not accomplish this ultimate goal in life.[12]

Part and parcel of being tried in this life is engaging with other people. If a person attempts to escape people by living in seclusion, the drawbacks will be greater. Take this example. A person wants to escape the possibility of contracting the flu, or any similar contagious virus. So he decides that he will avoid people at all costs and seclude himself to the four walls of his home. He may be successful in avoiding the flu, but in the meantime he is likely to develop a host of other disorders or unhealthy habits. Seclusion, especially for prolong periods, can be destructive to a person's physical, spiritual, and mental health.

Fifth, and more specifically, seclusion and isolation result in a number of spiritual illnesses. Engaging with the wrong people certainly has its negative effects on one's spiritual state, but so does living in isolation. One of the major spiritual ails that sometimes develops as a result of isolation is self-conceit. In detaching oneself from society, he may fall deeper into preconceived notions of society's shortcomings and weaknesses. Since he is detached from that, he does not have what they suffer from; thus, he may develop a sense of superiority as one who is presumably above the fray. Another vice that follows suit here is duplicity. Isolation can deceive a person into thinking that his virtue is greater than others. He is pious and detached from the world. Though he is detached from society, he implicitly wishes to be seen by society for those virtues and acts accordingly to gain that favorable view from them. His intentions may be swayed

---

[12] Ibid.

and falling into duplicity can be easier than what most may assume.

All in all, Islam rejects living in seclusion as a lifestyle in God's way. Al-Tabrasi commented in Majma' Al-Bayan on this matter by saying, "In our traditions, a prohibition on isolation is mentioned, meaning that an individual should not entirely disengage from people and groups."[13]

Monasticism is prohibited in Islam. We do not believe that wholesome living comes through isolating oneself from people and residing in a faraway mountain or monastery. It is narrated the Prophet said, "In my nation, there is no monasticism, hermitry, or silence [i.e. fasting from speaking]."[14]

In fact, Islam deems a person's journey to perfection and seeking the pleasure of his Lord to be contingent on his engagement and connection with people. This is also manifested in the fact that most rituals of worship are to be performed or recommended in a congregation.

BROTHERS AND EQUALS

Islam desires for us to connect and engage with people and deepen our connection with them through mutual respect and care. Beyond our blood-relatives, we look at people in one of two ways: brothers in faith or equals in humanity.

Equals in Humanity

Our religion does not discourage its followers from mixing with people from different walks of life, instead it promotes

[13] Al-Tabrasi, *Majma' Al-Bayan*, 10:164.
[14] Al-Sadouq, *Ma'ani Al-Akhbar*, 174.

it. The Holy Prophet and his disciples set this example throughout their lifetimes by befriending, working, and even marrying from people of different cultures, ethnicities, and backgrounds. Having diverse relationships has an impact on our state of mind, our way of life, and the fruits of our work both in this life and the next. Moreover, if we wish to spread goodness and godly values in this world then we cannot do so without connecting with people, that may, think differently or live differently than we do. By being that friend, neighbor, or colleague that is known for his or her impeccable moral character you may gain the trust and respect of your peers. Through that trust and respect you may very well be that influence that guides them towards a more wholesome and purposeful life.

The authentic tradition of Muawiya Ibn Wahab clearly explains how a person should deal with people in his community. He asked Imam Al-Sadiq, "What should we do amongst ourselves and our tribesman, as well as others?" Imam Al-Sadiq answered, "You must deliver what you are entrusted with, and provide testimony [whether it be] for or against them. Visit their ill ones and attend their funerals…"[15]

Even more than that, our faith instructs us to do good towards all people, Muslim and non-Muslim alike. God tells us to forge relationships characterized by good-doing towards non-Muslims, particularly those who do not express enmity to Islam and Muslims. God says in the Holy Quran,

---

[15] Al-Kulayni, *Al-Kafi*, 2:635.

God does not forbid you respecting those who have not made war against you on account of [your] religion, and have not driven you forth from your homes, that you show them kindness and deal with them justly; surely God loves the do-ers of justice. God only forbids you respecting those who made war upon you on account of [your] religion, and drove you forth from your homes and backed up [others] in your expulsion, that you make friends with them, and whoever makes friends with them, these are the unjust.[16]

This is contrary to some misinformed notions that some might have in which they justify disrespecting non-Muslims and not associating with them. How can a person deliver the message of Islam to those people if he does not establish effective and meaningful relationships with them? What is greater than disseminating the noble teachings of Islam through constructive dialogue and good words. This type of relationship is built on a host of standards and guidelines that God has prescribed in His divine teachings.

The first fundamental standard is respect for all people. God instructs people to respect one another. This respect should manifest itself in how we connect and treat one another. Mercy and compassion should be that focal point that brings us together. This is beautifully manifested in the teachings of the Imam Ali where he instructs Malik Al-Ashtar in his letter to him,

Habituate your heart to mercy for the subjects and let it be a source of kindness and affection for them. Surely, you must not act toward them like a ravaging beast who devours

---

[16] The Holy Quran. Chapter 60. [She that Needs to be Examined; Arabic: *Al-Mumtahina*]. Verse 9.

their food. Remember that they are of two types; either your brother in faith or equal in humanity.[17]

As the disciple and successor of the Holy Prophet, Imam Ali makes God's law clear. You are to look at another human being in one of two ways: he is your brother or your equal. We reject arrogance and favoritism. We promote equality and justice. We are brothers and equals, and we must honor this principle in all aspects of our lives.

The instructions to Malik Al-Ashtar are inclusive of Muslims and non-Muslims alike. It is not merely a call to generically feel sympathy or care about the general wellbeing of others, but rather for a person to make the qualities of care and empathy a part of who they are. Once those feelings are developed in the heart, they will dictate their action and conduct. A leader is a role model for his people. If his thoughts and emotions are dictated by compassion and mercy, then his citizens will follow suit and embrace these values in their daily lives.

The second standard that should govern our relationships with people is showing courtesy and politeness. Islam promotes people to exhibit good manners and upright behavior with all people. Dealing with others with good manners is a fundamentally necessary practice. It is our way of life. Moreover, Islam deems courtesy as an instance of intellect and wisdom. Soma'a narrates that Imam Al-Sadiq said, "Being courteous is one third of the intellect."[18]

---

[17] Al-Radi, *Nahj Al-Balagha*, 3:84.

[18] Al-Harrani, *Tohaf Al-'Oqool*, 366.

Abu Baseer narrates from Imam Al-Sadiq that his father Imam Al-Baqir said,

> *An Arab from the tribe of Tameem came to the Holy Prophet and told him, 'Advise me'. As part of the advice, the Prophet instructed him to 'love people, they will love you.'*[19]

Out of the spirit of being courteous and loving people, it is imperative to continue to be considerate of others' sensitivities and avoid instigating conflict. The ethics of Islam forbid conflict, debate, and controversy if it is not intended to effectively and meaningfully reveal the truth. Even when it does come to the idea of revealing the truth, there are limitations. One ought to be considerate of others by respecting their thoughts and opinions and not harming them. It is narrated that Imam Al-Sadiq said in this regard, "The Messenger of God said, 'God has commanded me to be considerate of people, as he commanded me to perform acts of worship.'"[20]

Brothers in Faith

Brothers in Faith are brothers in the way of God. They share the same godly values and principles in pursuit of God's pleasure and contentment. They share faith and creed, principle and thought, passion and empathy. This relationship is no less in value and significance than that had with blood relatives.

The narrations have described this as a relationship of brotherhood – the highest form in fact, because it is found-

---

[19] Al-Kulayni, Al-Kafi, 2:642.
[20] Ibid.

ed on faith in God. "A brother that your mother did not give birth to,"[21] Imam Ali describes the brother in faith.

The Holy Quran also refers to this concept of brotherhood, "The believers are but brethren, therefore make peace between your brethren and be careful of [your duty to] God that mercy may be had on you."[22]

This form of brotherhood is so great that it may even be more significant than some relationships with blood-relatives. Family relationships do not always persist, as was the case of some of God's prophets with their own families. Take the example of Prophet Noah and his son. Although they were of the same flesh and blood, the relationship terminated when Prophet Noah's son deviated from the way of God and became a disbeliever.

> *And Noah cried out to his Lord and said, 'My Lord, surely my son is of my family, and Your promise is surely true, and You are the most just of the judges.' He said, 'O Noah, surely he is not of your family; surely he is [the doer of] other than good deeds, therefore ask not of Me that of which you have no knowledge; surely I admonish you lest you may be of the ignorant.*[23]

The story of Noah demonstrates that family relationships can be severed when faith is compromised. However, brotherhood founded on faith is perpetual and thus gives it greater weight and value. Islam has always embraced the

---

21 Al-Laithi Al-Waseti, *Iyoun Al-Hikam wa Al-Mawa'idh*, 267.

22 The Holy Quran. Chapter 49. [The Inner Apartments; Arabic: *Al-Hujraat*]. Verse 10.

23 The Holy Quran. Chapter 11. [The Inner Apartments; Arabic: *Al-Hujraat*]. Verse 45-46.

idea of brotherhood amongst believers. At this point, we will move on to discuss brotherhood and what it entails of a strong foundation and the mutual responsibility needed to grow such an important relationship.

BROTHERHOOD

THE PILLARS OF BROTHERHOOD

Islam stresses faith-based brotherhood and fostering relationships with believers generally. Through the Holy Quran and the Prophet's tradition, God guides us to have this brotherhood built on a proper foundation so it may thrive, flourish, and produce good fruits. The following are some of the main pillars that make up the foundation for brotherhood in Islam.

Faith

The first pillar to build sound brotherhood in Islam is faith. The objective of this sacred relationship should be faith and loving God. Our narrations stress faith as opposed to friendships based on material things because relationships founded on worldly things are finite. It is narrated that Imam Ali said, "A brother earned in the way of God is the closest of people, and more merciful than mothers and fathers."[1] On another occasion the Imam also said that, "The

---

[1] Al-Laithy Al-Waseti, *Iyoun Al-Hukm wa Al-Mawaeith*, 55.

love between brothers in faith will endure, as its purpose is enduring."[2]

A relationship found on faith is more lasting because the mutual interest in the relationship is the love for God. The parties in the relationship will share a common love for their Lord and help one another achieve piety and advance in their faith. These mutual benefits are immortal as opposed to materialistic things where interests are more self-centered, may often diverge and result in conflict.

A relationship based in faith will only weaken if the faith fades away. It generates its strength from God as Imam Al-Baqir explains in his beautiful narration, "Whoever gains a brother in God – one who believes in God and is loyal in brotherhood as a means to seek God's pleasure – will gain a beam of divine light."[3] By the same token, the traditions warned against brotherhood being built on worldly interests because it is inevitable where interests will cause deviation and conflict will arise. The relationship will transform from brotherhood to enmity. And even if it is the case where that sort of brotherhood will survive in this life, it will turn to enmity in the hereafter. Imam Ali said,

> *People are brothers… any brotherhood that is not in the way of God is enmity. This is what the Almighty refers to, 'The friends shall on that day be enemies one to another, except the righteous.'*[4]

---

[2] Ibid.

[3] Al-Harrani, *Tohaf Al-'Oqool*, 295.

[4] Al-Majlisi, *Bihar Al-Anwar*, 71:165.

If worldly interests, even those that are permissible, are not sufficient to be a foundation for this sacred relationship, it is even more critical for brotherhood not to be based on heedlessness and vice. Even if on the surface of this relationship there is brotherhood and love, in essence it merely just holds evil, enmity, and hatred. True brotherhood is one that will render happiness in both this life and hereafter.

However, if heedlessness is the link between people, then this connection will naturally render an undesirable place in one's afterlife – God's displeasure and punishment. Imam Ali was asked about who is a wicked friend, he replied, "One who beautifies to you the disobedience of God."[5] Sorrow and regret is the outcome of these unwise relationships. Though a person may be simply looking at the now, what is fun and what feels good, if they are to look ahead they would wish that they would not have had such baseless friendships.

> *The Day that the wrong-doer will bite at his hands, he will say, oh! would that I had taken a [straight] path with the Messenger! Ah, woe is me! Would that I had never taken such a one for a friend. Certainly he led me astray from the reminder after it had come to me; and Satan fails to aid man.*[6]

The Holy Household tied this relationship to faith, and the importance of building brotherly bonds based on values and principles. It is a prophetic tradition to promote this type of brotherhood and friendship because of its enormous bene-

[5] Al-Sadouq, *Man La Yahdaruh Al-Faqih*, 4:383.
[6] The Holy Quran. Chapter 25. [The Criterion; Arabic: *Al-Furqaan*]. Verse 27-29.

21

fit, as it leads to one's stability, peace of mind, and happiness. Imam Al-Sadiq is narrated to have said,

> *Increase your friends in this world, for they are useful in this life and hereafter. In this life, they will [help] fulfill needs, and in the hereafter the people of hellfire said, 'So we have no intercessors, nor a true friend.'* [7]

When the people of hellfire remember their intercessors and true friends, certainly this is indicative that these people have a role in saving a person from hellfire. Moreover, it is symptomatic of a special type of friendship and brotherhood such that its effect alleviates punishment. We cannot comprehend this impact unless the relationship is found on faith, which is narrated by Imam Al-Sadiq,

> *Increase your brothers for every brother has an accepted prayer... Increase your brothers for every brother will be an intercessor... Increase your brotherhood with the believers for they have a status with God that He will reward them for on the Day of Judgement.* [8]

Intellect

One of the greatest creations of God was the intellect of man. The role of the intellect in leading a person to the truth is beyond the scope of this discussion. What is pertinent here is the intellect's role in faith-based brotherhood.

The intellect is one of the key pillars that contributes to the durability and sustainability of this relationship. It plays a vital role in preserving this sacred institution by protecting it from anything that offends it or undermines it. Further-

---

[7] Al-Sadouq, *Musadaqat Al-Ikhwan*, 46.

[8] Al-Hur Al-Amili, *Wasa'el Al-Shia*, 8:408.

more, a person desires to benefit from this relationship which cannot truly take place without an intellectual dynamic. We need our brothers to be intellectual to help guide us to what is best. By intellectual it does not necessarily translate to an elitist form of academism nor is it a style of abstract philosophy and rhetoric. A person who is characteristic of using and engaging his intellect is one who is able to think through situations, rationalize, and endure the hardships of life. By that token, he is able to help his brother to do the same. Imam Al-Sadiq refers to this in his narration,

> *Brothers are three; the first is like nutrition that is needed at all times which is the intellectual, the second is like a disease who is the fool, and the third is like the medicine who is the reasonable.*[9]

An intellectual person advises, guides, supports, and aids one during difficult times. On the contrary, an unintellectual individual can lead one into trouble, be it inadvertently or purposefully. It is important that if we wish to be intellectual and move ourselves in the right direction that we surround ourselves with others that have the same focus and drive. When we do that we set up mutually beneficial relationships that add value to our lives and keep us on track. Our faith promotes this idea of engagement, sharing thoughts and ideas, and investing in one another's intellect.

This is what Islam advocates for – building relationships on these foundations. Only through this collective thought and shared experiences can a righteous community rise and thrive. This is required in order to bring forth that host of

---

[9] Al-Harrani, *Tohaf Al-'Oqool*, 323.

elements that are required to render real benefit. The intellect is one of those crucial elements. To merely consult others, appreciating their knowledge and experience, itself is an admirable thing. Imam Al-Sadiq narrates,

> The Messenger of God said, 'Consulting an intellectual advisor shows maturity and brings blessings and success granted by God. If an intellectual advisor provides you with advice, beware of rejecting [the advice and acting to the contrary] for it will render damage.[10]

In another narration, Imam Al-Sadiq shows the role of the intellectual in addition to other elements related to seeking advice and consultation. Through this narration, the connection between brotherhood, faith, intellect, and virtue becomes more apparent. Al-Halabi narrates that Imam Al-Sadiq said,

> Advice is only [effective if it is applied] within its limitations. One needs to understand it with its limitations, otherwise its harm will greatly outweigh its benefits for the advisee.
> First, the advisor should be an intellectual.
> Second, he should be free and religious.
> Third, he should be a friend and brother.
> Fourth, you should reveal your secrets to him such that his knowledge of them becomes like yours, but he should conceal and hide them.
> If he was an intellectual, you will benefit from his advice.
> If he was free and religious, he will struggle diligently to advise you.

---

[10] Al-Barqi, *Al-Mahasin*, 2:602.

If he was a friend and brother, he will conceal the secrets you reveal to him.

If you reveal your secrets such that his knowledge of them becomes like yours, the consultation and advice will be complete.[11]

This noble narration highlights the deep value that lies in a person seeking the advice of an intellectual in addition to the strong bond between brotherhood, faith, and virtue.

Virtue

Friendship and brotherhood have a powerful impact on a person. We take from those around us, especially in terms of habits, virtue and vice. Consequently, a person's path to success and excellence relies much on the presence of common noble virtues with those around him. The closer a person is to you the more applicable this principle is.

Man's primary objective is the pursuit of happiness – striving and reaching his excellence. This cannot come to fruition except through virtue and righteousness. To do that, we have to take it upon ourselves to live in wholesome environments. Our communities must be characteristic of goodness and virtue so that we may continue to be nurtured by godly values and principles. If our environment is not the kind that will help us grow in the right direction, then we should not expect ourselves to develop towards the goals we set to achieve.

To demonstrate the significance of the influence of our environment, particularly as it is dictated by friends, we revisit a narration by Imam Al-Sadiq from the Holy Prophet. "The

---

[11] Ibid.

Messenger of God says, 'Man is on the religion of his friend… one needs to pay attention to whom he befriends.'"[12]

Imam Ali advised his son Imam Hassan in his will about the people he should surround himself with. His advice to his own son is universally applied to all sons and daughters. "Associate with the people of goodness, you will be from them. And disassociate from the people of evil, you will be far from them."[13]

There are plenty of narrations that urge the believers to select friends and companions who carry good attributes and high morals and, at the same time, to stay away from those who possess ill manners. As human beings we are deeply affected by those around us. It reflects who we are, not merely as a show of good or bad judgment in choosing friends, but as a practical impact on our own character. If the friends we choose are not a reflection of what we would like to see in ourselves, we are bound to see ourselves detrimented in one way or another. Hannan Ibn Sudair narrates that Imam Al-Baqir said,

> Do not associate or take as a brother four [types of people]: a fool, a miser, a coward, and a liar. As for a fool, he desires to help you but he will in turn harm you. As for a miser, he will take from you and not give. As for a coward, he will desert you and his parents. As for a liar, he [may at times] tell the truth, [but still] should not be believed.

---

[12] Al-Majlisi, *Bihar Al-Anwar*, 71:192.
[13] Al-Radi, *Nahj Al-Balagha*, 3:52.

The traditions are explicit in warning against the companionship of such individuals because they will render greater harm than good. A person ought to seek moral benefit, not material or monetary gain, from his brothers and friends. Imam Al-Sadiq speaks to that when he quotes the Holy Prophet to have said, "The happiest people are those who associate with honorable people."[14]

True brotherhood is deep and meaningful. Its mutual engagement is usually both horizontal and vertical – doing many things together, while being able to have a lot quality in one particular area. Essentially, it is not what we often find in acquaintances of basic small talk and superficial association. Given the connection and depth involved in brotherhood, we need to be aware of our responsibilities to one another. First, a person needs to be wise in selecting his brothers and friends. Second, a person needs to put the time and effort to maintain that brotherhood because of the value it holds. At this point, it is worthwhile to discuss a few additional points on brotherhood and friendship.

Trying Friends. God has instructed the believers to try friends before taking them as brothers and companions. A person needs to proceed with caution in forging new relationships and opening up to new friends, and take time to examine the likelihood of success in the relationship. Imam Ali says, "Put forth tests and thorough examinations when selecting your brothers. Otherwise, necessity will compel you to associate with the wicked."[15]

---

[14] Al-Sadouq, *Man La Yahdaruh Al-Faqih*, 4:395.
[15] Al-Laithy Al-Wasti, Iyoun Al-Hukm wa Al-Mawaeith, 370.

To assess the likelihood of success in the relationship, a person must determine whether the relationship was built on the proper pillars, as we discussed previously. Imam Al-Sadiq said,

> Try your brothers with two traits. If they have [the two traits, take them as brothers]; otherwise be sure to stay far away. [First] is maintaining prayers on time and [second] is doing good towards brothers in [times] of hardship and ease.[16]

Perhaps, in mentioning these two characteristics, the Imam is referring to two important things. First, a person who is religious about performing his timely prayers is one who displays consistency, commitment, and constancy. Second, a person who does good towards his brothers is one who is loyal, dependable, and trustworthy. These characteristics are necessary for any lasting relationship.

Seriousness of the Relationship. It is a grave mistake to think that having a brother and companion is only for enjoyment. Yes, one of the objectives of companionship is for the friends to hang out, relax, and have a good time. That is an important dimension to the relationship. But it should not be the only dimension of the relationship. If it is it could be at the cost of one's growth and development, especially intellectually and spiritually. It could render the relationship to be one that is worldly driven where the objective is mere entertainment. As we mentioned, entertainment and fun will eventually fade and will be replaced with conflict and harm.

---

[16] Al-Kulayni, Al-Kafi, 2:672.

Thus, seriousness in a relationship is essential. What is meant by seriousness is that a person searches for that which will benefit his brother, whether he finds it desirable or not. It is this type of relationship that the noble narrations focus on. A relationship ought to help a person propel by reaching his Lord, not digress in disgrace. The Commander of the Faithful Imam Ali said, "The best of your brothers is he who propels you into God's obedience."[17] The connection is clear. A true brother brings you closer to God. The Prophet also said, "The best of your brothers is the one who guides you to your shortcomings."[18]

Continuity of the Relationship. In order for a relationship to continue and render its fruits, it must be sustained and not severed or compromised. Furthermore, its continuity should not be merely based on a give-and-take setup. A believer should not adopt a mindset of reciprocating the relationship such that he will only invest in it if the other party is reaching out. Islam teaches us to take the initiative in reaching out to our brothers and friends in order to maintain our bond with them. We must take the first step. We must make it a priority. We must take the lead as Imam Ali advises, "Obey your brother even if he doesn't obey you, and connect with him even if he does not reach out to you."[19]

---

[17] Al-Laithi Al-Waseti, *Iyoun Al-Hikam wa Al-Mawa'idh*, 238.

[18] Al-Reyshahri, *Mizan Al-Hikma*, 1:46.

[19] Al-Laithi Al-Waseti, *Iyoun Al-Hikam wa Al-Mawa'idh*, 79.

RIGHTS AND OBLIGATIONS

In every relationship, there are rights and obligations. The deeper the relationship is, the more rights and obligations there will be. It is not necessary that the rights and obligations are equally shared between the two parties. In some relationships, one party might have more rights than the other while the other party might have more obligations. For example, in the parent-child relationship, the parents have more rights than their children and the children have greater obligations towards their parents.

God constructed the relationship between the believers to be of brotherhood which render rights and obligations. God desires for the believer to offer more and take less, and urges us to do good and give generously. We ought to carry this spirit in our transactions with our brothers in faith, because it reflects a way of living that is greater than oneself. If our trust is in God then we would have no trouble giving, because we know that our reward is from Him and Him alone. Giving, and giving generously, is essentially for God at the end of the day. We are merely agents or instruments of God to provide sustenance towards one another. True sustenance is determined and decreed by God alone. In light of that, it is our choice to be part of that positively or to be a hindrance in the process. And that is the blessing and burden of free will, and ultimately of our life on Earth.

Affection and Love

Of the most important rights amongst brothers are love and affection. Brotherhood cannot survive without love and affection. There are some unhealthy relationships, based either on general socialization or business gains, that do not require this. However, because brotherhood is rooted in religion and founded on faith, love is an essential pillar necessary for the success of the relationship. The traditions of the Prophet and his disciples linked the element of love and affection in brotherhood to faith itself.

It is narrated that Imam Al-Sadiq has said, "Part of a man's love for his religion is his love for his brothers."[20] As a person's faith strengthens, his love for his brothers should amplify. A rise in that love is a sign of increasing faith as is mentioned by the Holy Prophet. "The love for a believer is one of the greatest reasons for faith."[21]

If a person does not feel a sense of affection and affinity towards his brothers, then that brotherhood will be compromised. The Commander of the Faithful says, "If you do not love your brother, you are not his brother."[22] Loving your brother and showing affection towards him is part and parcel of the brotherhood that God has established amongst the believers. It might be argued that love and affection is a feeling that a person cannot create or control. Thus, how can a person be mandated to have this feeling or express it to others?

In answering this question, we need to realize that actions are of two types. External actions that a person performs and displays and internal actions that a person might decide to conceal. With respect to internal actions, the heart engages in these actions and can choose to conceal them from the

---

[20] Al-Sadouq, *Al-Khisal*, 3.

[21] Al-Majlisi, *Bihar Al-Anwar*, 71:281.

[22] Al-Harrani, *Tohaf Al-'Oqool*, 173.

outside such that they go unnoticed by others. This is the case with duplicity, arrogance, and envy. The reality of these issues, as in what really exists, is internal in a person's heart and is not necessarily expressed on the outside. A person lives these feelings and can choose to reveal them or not. Nonetheless, a person is accountable for these feelings and will be judged for them by God. The Holy Quran expresses that a person will be judged for what transpires in his heart and soul as is the case with all other organs, "Follow not that of which you have not the knowledge; surely the hearing and the sight and the heart, all of these, shall be questioned about that."[23]

Consequently, a person ought to control his emotions and feelings and connect them to his Lord. As a result, a person who is committed to his faith will not be able to express love and affection to the enemies of God.

> *You shall not find a people who believe in God and the latter day befriending those who act in opposition to God and His Messenger, even though they were their (own) fathers, or their sons, or their brothers, or their kinsfolk; these are they into whose hearts He has impressed faith, and whom He has strengthened with an inspiration from Him: and He will cause them to enter gardens beneath which rivers flow, abiding therein; God is well-pleased with them and they are well-pleased with Him these are God's party: now surely the party of God are the successful ones.*[24]

---

[23] The Holy Quran. Chapter 17. [The Night Journey; Arabic: *Al-Israa'*]. Verse 36.
[24] The Holy Quran. Chapter 58. [The Pleading Woman; Arabic: *Al-Mujaadila*]. Verse 22.

It is imperative for a believer to love and hate in the way of God. If a person does not feel a sense of affection to his brothers in faith, he should examine why that love is lacking and reconsider his position. Loving is not optional for the believer. If it is something in the way of God, truly, you will have a love for it. The thought and the feeling will be connected. However, if the feeling is not there automatically there must be time given to understand the thought to allow for the feeling to develop with it.

Factors that Affect Love and Affection

After establishing the correlation between one's faith and his love for believers, a person should strive to continuously strengthen his affection towards his brothers. If the love and affection between the believers is reduced, brotherhood will be compromised, and faith will be weakened. The Prophet warned the believers from some of the factors that weaken or reduce love and affection including the following.

Decency. Linguistically, decency means 'constriction and modesty'. The traditions of the Holy Household mention that decency and modesty between the believers is one of the major factors that contributes to the survival and affection between the believers. Although brotherhood is an intimate relationship where formalities should be alleviated to a certain extent, decency should remain strong because it will ensure proper conduct. If decency fades away, the companions will be more susceptible to problems that can compromise their brotherhood. The narrations of the Ahlulbayt warned against this issue. Imam Al-Sadiq says,

Decency should not be removed between you and your broth-er, keep some of it. The removal of decency is the removal of modesty and the survival of decency is the survival of love.[25]

Restraining the Tongue. As human beings, we can pos-sess some of the greatest levels of self-restraint and patience during trial and hardship. At other times, however, we can lose our cool or even explode at some of the most trivial things. A person needs to be cautious in his dealings with his brothers by restraining his tongue. An ill tongue can det-riment the relationship by reducing the love between broth-ers. In fact, it can escalate and result in hatred and spite. All it takes is one word in the heat of the moment to ruin a rela-tionship of years.

A person needs to be conscious of this matter and be care-ful in how he speaks and addresses his fellow brothers. He should refrain from addressing certain matters that irritate or provoke them. Restraining the tongue will go a long way in avoiding unnecessary problems and preserving the broth-erhood. This does not mean that you do not talk openly with your brothers, but instead are considerate of them and do not do things in spite of them. It is a reflection of one's care and respect for others. Imam Zain Al-Abideen touches on this issue when he says, "[If you] restrain your tongue, you will maintain your brothers [and their trust]."[26]

Preserving the Rights of Brotherhood. As a true brother you should refrain from thinking or feeling that you have the upper hand in your relationship. You should never take the other side for granted. Be one who is motivated to offer

[25] Al-Harrani, *Tohaf Al-'Oqool*, 370.
[26] Al-Tabrasi, *Al-Ihtijaj*, 2:52.

more for his brothers because of his care and commitment to them. Again, it is vital that we do not take our brotherhood for granted at any point. Some may mistakenly believe that because the relationship is well established and has been existent for years that they are somehow fine to slack off in the relationship. Such an outlook is a recipe for disaster and will cause that brotherhood to fail. No matter how strong and firm the brotherhood becomes, its longevity is contingent on both parties appreciating, embracing, and fulfilling their duties to one another. Imam Ali said,

> *Do not squander the rights of your brother by relying [on the assumption] that the good relationship between you and him is unbreakable, for a person is not your brother if you squander his rights.*[27]

Virtuous Conduct. Virtues and manners must dominate the relationship. Compassion must be the foundation for this relationship. When compassion, justice, and equity are present, the affection amongst the brothers will be crystalized and cemented. Conversely, if it is lacking, love will dissipate and worse, hatred will replace it, which will ruin the most amazing relationship that God has created between the believers. It is narrated that Imam Al-Sadiq said,

> *Brothers require three traits [in their relationship] among themselves. If they do not utilize [these three traits], they will differ and have enmity towards one another. [These traits are] equity, compassion, and lack of envy.*[28]

---

[27] Al-Sadouq, *Man La Yahdaruh Al-Faqih*, 4:392.
[28] Al-Harrani, *Tohaf Al-'Oqool*, 323.

These virtues highlighted by the Imam are linked back to the notion of giving. Equity and justice are amongst the best virtues that repel a person from squandering other people's rights and drive him to give others their due right. Compassion is what leads to an increase in giving, doing good, and benevolence. Negating envy is equally essential because envy renders ill will. Moreover, an envious person usually becomes malevolent to others, which will only render further hate and ill will.

In addition to these specific desirable virtues, a person must adhere to general good conduct in his transactions with his brothers. He should not drop the veil of modesty and only exemplify the utmost respect to his brothers. One should do anything in his capacity to encompass his brothers, be considerate of their feelings, and show love and affection towards them.

Loving the Believers

Supplications. To cultivate love for the believers and obtain reciprocated affection, one must resort to his Lord. The Holy Quran mentions that a person needs to refer to God in both cases. God is the owner of the heart. He is the One that turns and shapes the heart as He wills. Through connecting and calling onto Him, a person is able to penetrate people's hearts and also fill his own heart with love for others. "Surely [as for] those who believe and do good deeds, for them will God bring about love."[29] Imam Al-Sadiq comments on this holy verse,

---

[29] The Holy Quran. Chapter 19. [Mary; Arabic: *Maryan*]. Verse 96.

> *The reason for the revelation of this verse is that the Com-*
> *mander of the Faithful was sitting before the Messenger of*
> *God who said, 'say O' Ali, O' Lord instill my love in the*
> *hearts of the believers.' Thus God revealed, 'Surely [as for]*
> *those who believe and do good deeds, for them will God*
> *bring about love.'* [30]

God also teaches us to love others by supplicating for them. The following is a supplication in the Holy Quran teaching us how to supplicate for our brethren.

> *And those who come after them say, 'Our Lord forgive us*
> *and those of our brethren who had precedence of us in faith,*
> *and do not allow any spite to remain in our hearts towards*
> *those who believe, our Lord surely you art Kind, Merci-*
> *ful.* [31]

No doubt, one of the factors that garners the love of the believers is supplicating for them and wishing them well. It shows them you genuinely care for them. Thus, God will bless you with their love and affection.

Gifting. The traditions of Ahlulbayt urge the believers to engage in gifting to earn love and compassion. There numerous traditions that point to this principle – gifting is one of the sources of love.

The Prophet says, "Gifting renders love. Gift [one another] for it removes grudges."[32] It is important to mention that the value of a gift in these traditions is not measured by its cost or quantity, but rather by it sentimental value. A person

---

[30] Al-Qummi, *Tafseer Al-Qummi*, 2:56.

[31] The Holy Quran. Chapter 59. [The Exile; Arabic: *Al-Hashr*]. Verse 10.

[32] Al-Kulayni, *Al-Kafi*, 5:144.

should continuously offer gifts to his brothers and companions, even if it is something simple, in order to show care and love. The Messenger of God adds, "Gift, for a gift removes impurities, and alleviates the grudges of enmity and spite."[33] The receiver should embrace these gifts and appreciate their sentimental value. A person receiving a gift should never belittle a gift because it is not grand or expensive. The value of the gift is in the thought and intention behind it.

Expressing Love. One of the factors that contributes to the growth and continuity of love in brotherhood is expressing that very love. As obvious as we may think that our thoughts and feelings are, at the end of the day they are thoughts and feelings. They are internal things that could not be known without expression. And even if they are known without consciously expressing them, we reaffirm them with those we love when we do. People do not know how much you care until you tell them or better yet show them that you do. The mere expression of care, love, and compassion can boost your loved ones' spirits and self-worth, because they are reminded of how much you appreciate and love them. It is narrated in Al-Mahasin that Imam Al-Baqir and Imam Al-Sadiq were sitting down with company in a mosque when a man passed by. One of the persons directed himself to the Imams and said, "By God I love this man..." Imam Al-Baqir told him, "Surely, you should inform him, for that will sustain affection and is good for companionship."[34]

---

[33] Ibid.
[34] Al-Barqi, *Al-Mahasin*, 1:266.

Support and Cooperation

Support and cooperation amongst brothers is a right that we must all observe. This is a principle that God mandates on the believers. It is not enough to merely call each other brothers without actually being there for one another and extending that helping hand. A Muslim must be concerned and invested in general affairs of his community. One ought to live this day in and day out. Otherwise, he is not truly a Muslim. Imam Al-Sadiq said, "Whoever is not concerned with the affairs of the Muslims, is not one of them."[35]

A person that wants to maintain his status as a Muslim must live their problems, issues, and challenges. Furthermore, he should take steps to provide support within his capacity. Imam Al-Sadiq narrates on the behalf of the Prophet, "Whoever hears a calling, 'Oh Muslims!', and does not answer, is not a Muslim."[36]

Whether it is substantial monetary support – helping a needy family buy furniture for their home – or moral support like supplicating for another brother, support must be provided. A person who lives his days only concerned about his own livelihood and is apathetic to the state of his community, cannot claim to be a true Muslim. A Muslim must feel a sense of ongoing responsibility towards his brothers. He will one-day face adversity or be inflicted with a calamity where he will need a shoulder to lean on. If he wants someone to answer his plea for help, he needs to be there for people during their challenging times and moments of sor-

---

[35] Al-Kulayni, *Al-Kafi*, 2:164.
[36] Ibid.

row. What is better than being a means to alleviate someone's pain and fulfill his need?

Prophetic tradition shows that offering brothers support is not only recommended, it is obligatory. It is necessary in order for the community to reach the virtuous state desired by God. The Prophet said,

> *A Muslim is the brother of a Muslim. He does not oppress, abandon, or betray him. It is incumbent on Muslims to strive in connecting and cooperate in showing sympathy and empathy to people in need, and to show sympathy to one another so that you can be as God commanded you, 'merciful amongst yourselves...' and disheartened for what you do not know of [each other's tragedies.] [Thus you may be] just like the Ansar [who aided the Holy Prophet] during [his] time.*[37]

The notion of support and help must be based in faith and piety. Thus, a Muslim cannot support an oppressor just because he is a Muslim. Alternatively, the deviant Muslim should be guided to return to the righteous path. God states in the Holy Quran, "Help one another in goodness and piety, and do not help one another in sin and aggression; and be careful of [your duty to] God; surely God is severe in requiting [evil]."[38]

Advice

Brotherhood in faith is a godly relationship that is not built on worldly interests. A believer's primary concern is to invest in this relationship as a vehicle to reach God. Conse-

---

[37] Al-Kulayni, *Al-Kafi*, 2:174.
[38] The Holy Quran. Chapter 5. [The Table; Arabic: *Al-Maaida*]. Verse 2.

quently, this relationship becomes about fostering connections and collaboration rather than competition and rivalry.

A believer must help his fellow brother rise with him by providing enlightening advice. Offering advice is one of the best deeds and most desirable to God. It is narrated by the Prophet, "The greatest people in status with God on Judgment Day are those who walk on earth [offering] advice to His people."[39] God mandated on the believers to provide advice to one another. Imam Al-Sadiq said, "A believer is entitled to receive advice from the believers in privacy and public."[40]

It is better to be proactive and let a brother know that you are there to help them. When a person observes another believer engaged in a flawed opinion or action, he should stop and provide some guidance to prevent his brother from falling into committing the wrong. Islam views any shortcoming in a person as a shortcoming of the entire community. The responsibility to remedy those weaknesses and turn them into strengths is on the shoulders of the community. This falls under the umbrella of enjoining in good and forbidding evil, which is an essential mandate on all believers. We do not take this responsibility lightly as God says in the Holy Quran, "I swear by time. Most surely man is in loss, except those who believe and do good, and enjoin on each other truth, and enjoin on each other patience."[41] At this juncture, it is important to address the following two points.

---

[39] Al-Kulayni, *Al-Kafi*, 2:208.

[40] Ibid.

[41] The Holy Quran. Chapter 103. [The Declining Day; Arabic: *Al-'Asr*]. Verse 1-3.

First, a person should be careful not to allow for unnecessary social courtesies to seep into his advice. Advice should not be compromised at the cost of courtesies. If one observes a wrong and knows he can offer effective guidance, he should not hesitate. Imam Ali addresses this particular point, "The best of brothers is the least artificial in his advice."[42] The key is effectiveness though, while being polite and kind.

One who abandons his brother by not supplying him with useful advice is in fact harming him. A real brother will provide authentic advice that can bring his brother back on track. Being silent in the face of wrong is a betrayal to one's brother. Imam Al-Sadiq said in that regards, "Whoever observes a brother engaged in something he abhors and does not stop him, when he is able, has betrayed [his brother]."[43]

Second, an advisee must accept the advice from his brother and friend when it conflicts with his desires or hurts his feelings. A person should not be hurt by a genuine brother who wishes well for him. And even if he is hurt by the truth, he needs to readjust and adapt to it. Brotherhood is about helping each other through and showing one another a path towards what is best. It is about openness and being genuine, not walking on eggshells to make sure no one gets offended. Of course, as we mentioned earlier the approach needs to be kind, polite, and most importantly effective. It will not be effective if it is overly courteous and superficial, nor would it be effective if it is too blunt and insensitive. In the end it is all for the purpose of becoming closer to God

---

[42] Al-Laithy Al-Waseti, *Iyoun Al-Hukm wa Al-Maweith*, 239.
[43] Al-Sadouq, *Al-Amaali*, 343.

as Imam Ali has said, "The best of your brothers is he who propels you into God's obedience."[44]

Honor and Respect

Another important right that a believer has in brotherhood is to be honored and respected by his brother. The honor and dignity of brothers is one. By virtue of their brotherhood, if one is dishonored or disgraced, the other is implicated as well. Thus, it is of the utmost priority to respect people and their dignity. As Muslims, the most sanctified place on God's earth is the Ka'ba – the first house of God. Imam Al-Sadiq proclaims that "the believer has greater sanctity than the Ka'ba,"[45] itself. The status of the believer with God is a lofty one that ought to be appreciated and revered.

We should be reminded that the respect we afford people should not be based on their influence, wealth, or power. It is imperative that we deal with people, whether they are rich or poor, powerful or weak, based on the principles of our faith. There are striking narrations that warn against insulting and harming a believer. It is narrated that Imam Al-Sadiq said, "Whoever insults a believer, indigent or not, God the Almighty will scorn and abhor him until he retracts from his insults."[46] It is also narrated from Al-Ma'aly Ibn Khanees that Imam Al-Sadiq said,

---

[44] Al-Laithy Al-Waseti, *Iyoun Al-Hukm wa Al-Maweith*, 238.
[45] Al-Sadouq, *Al-Khisal*, 27.
[46] Al-Kulayni, *Al-Kafi*, 2:351.

God, the most Blessed and High, says, 'Whoever insults a pious man has dedicated himself to wage war against Me, and I am the swiftest in supporting my pious companions.'[47]

The disparity amongst people in matters of wealth, knowledge, and influence is decreed by God. In his wisdom, God created this disparity so that life can take its natural course where people are in need of one another. People who are blessed must not become arrogant and degrade those that are less fortunate. The honor of the believer is given to him by God, so the believer must be dignified and honored for that. A believer respecting his fellow brother is in fact revering his faith. As a person elevates in his faith, he will increase in his respect for the faithful. Imam Al-Sadiq said, "Whoever glorifies his faith, glorifies his brothers. Whoever disparages his faith, disparages his brothers."[48]

Fulfilling the Needs of Brothers

One of the manifestations of brotherhood is feeling a sense of responsibility towards your brother. Brotherhood ceases to exist if the brothers do not share a mutual duty to support one another. Islam does not embrace a person who claims to be Muslim but he does not care about his brethren and is indifferent to their needs. On the contrary, irresponsibility is the way of the disbelievers as God indicates in the Holy Quran,

And when it is said to them, spend out of what God has given you, those who disbelieve say to those who believe, shall

---

[47] Ibid.
[48] Al-Tousi, *Al-Amaali*, 98.

we feed him whom, if God please, He could feed? You are
in naught but clear error.[49]

In creating disparities amongst people, God tests us with
each another. It is part of his divine plan in testing mankind.
His Wisdom dictated that people depend on each other for
various monetary and non-monetary necessities. In addition
to being a trial in His obedience, this scheme results in people building bridges and fostering brotherhood. In light of
this, a few points need to be highlighted.

Importance of Relying on Brothers. Everyone faces challenges in life, be it monetary, social, or moral. In the face of
adversity, one should not abstain from utilizing people's
help and aid to resolve his issues. It is this collaboration
amongst brothers that bolsters their social bond and grants
them strength to cope with adversity. Imam Al-Sadiq said,
"If one of you is pressed with difficulty, make your brother
aware and do not just rely on yourself."[50]

Some might misconstrue seeking others for help as the an-
tithesis of depending on God. This is wrong. Submitting to
divine instructions cannot conflict with depending on the
Lord. God instructs us to lean on our faithful brothers for
our needs. Resorting to people for assistance is submitting
to God's orders, which is essentially depending on Him.

Fulfilling the Need Before the Request. One of the obligations that a believer has towards his brother is to visit him
and be attentive to his needs. A person should be proactive
and not wait to be sought for help. Just like how a respon-

---

[49] The Holy Quran. Chapter 36. [Yaseen; Arabic: *Yaseen*]. Verse 47.
[50] Al-Kulayni, *Al-Kafi*, 4:49.

sible person is proactive towards his own family in attending to their needs and resolving their problems, whether they requested from him or not, he should act in the same manner with his brothers. Indeed, fulfilling a need for a brother before being sought is greater in God's eyes. Imam Ali comments on this matter beautifully, "You should not burden your brother to ask when you know his need." [51]

Striving to Fulfill People's Needs. It is not necessary that one is able to fulfill a brother's need directly. Incapacity to directly address a need does not alleviate the duty. A person can strive to help his brother indirectly by pursuing other means. Striving and pursuing, regardless of the outcome, will render recompense from the Divine.

Striving in itself is very positive. It reassures the person in need that someone cares for him and is there to provide support. That in itself will bolster the brotherhood. It is narrated that Imam Al-Sadiq said,

> When a servant strives in [fulfilling] the need of his faithful brother, God assigns him two angels, one on his right and the other on his left, supplicating to his Lord for forgiveness and to fulfill his needs...[52]

Effects of not Fulfilling a Brother's Need. God warned people from failing to fulfill their brothers' needs. It is disobedience that renders the severing of His guardianship. What is worse than severing one's relationship with God? Falling out of God's grace is no small matter. Whoever is not blessed with God being his guardian will be doomed

---

[51] Al-Majlisi, *Bihar Al-Anwar*, 71:166.
[52] Ibid.

with Satan as his custodian. Imam Al-Kadhim said, "Whoever is pursued by a brother for refuge in some of his matters and does not answer the calling when he is capable has severed God's guardianship."[53] Brotherhood is not to be dealt with lightly. It is a great responsibility, as it renders tremendous benefit and blessing. That benefit and blessing comes directly from God, as the relationship is founded on that shared principle and faith.

---

[53] Al-Kulayni, *Al-Kafi*, 2:367.

MARRIAGE

In the name of God, the most Beneficent, the most Merciful

And of His signs is that he created for you from yourselves mates that you may find tranquility in them; and he placed affection and mercy between you. Indeed, in that are sings for a people who give thought.[1]

The marvel of marriage has occupied humanity for centuries. Many people have attempted to understand the nature and essence of this relationship. Some have characterized it as solely an animalistic relationship that is found to satisfy sexual desires. Others have rejected this as an oversimplification and have advocated for a more holistic understanding of all aspects of marriage. Meanwhile, there are some that have committed their time to establishing laws and regulations that can institutionalize this relationship. We attempt to shed light on some of the important points related to this topic and reach beneficial conclusions.

Amongst the most important points are:

- What is the Islamic perspective on marriage?

---

[1] The Holy Quran. Chapter 30. [The Romans; Arabic: *Al-Rum*]. Verse 21.

- What are the benefits of marriage?
- How do we adjust our lives to the principles of our faith regarding marriage?

THE ISLAMIC PERSPECTIVE

In Islam, there are two primary issues in the domain of male-female relationships beyond platonic professional interactions. Those are sexual intimacy and the secret in creation, or reproduction. Both of these topics are related and go hand in hand but are also looked at as independent subjects.

Sexual desire is embedded in our human nature. It falls within our basic needs, along with food and shelter. God had ordained for the Islamic rules and applications to be compatible with human nature. God's law does not conflict with our nature, it merely gives us regulation to satisfy our desires while observing our objective and purpose as human beings. Islam does not frown up or reject sexual desire. It does not expect its followers to observe abstinence. Instead, it encourages people to fulfill their desires through the proper means, which is marriage. If it is not possible to get married, then patience is advised. However, the view on sexual desire is that it is a natural part of who we are as human beings and it should be channeled and fulfilled but of course in the proper way. Take the example of food and drink. No one will deny that every human being has to eat and drink to survive; however, in order to lead a healthy lifestyle there are certain foods you eat and certain foods you don't. There are times of the day that are better to eat in and there are times, like late at night, that you should not.

Thus, you will find that Islam encompasses this desire and merely regulates it for a healthy wholesome lifestyle, just like we do with food, exercise and diet.

The secret in creation lies in the reproduction and proliferation of mankind which allows for the survival of life on this planet. This process is exclusively dependent on the relationship between man and woman. Therefore, Islam views the relationship between the two genders as the proper and necessary avenue for the survival of mankind. It is the will of God to have his creations worship Him as indicated in the Holy Quran, "And I have not created the jinn and mankind except so that they worship me."[2]

This notion becomes the basis for Islam's outlook on sex, which we will discuss later on in this chapter.

In light of discussing Islam's philosophy on marriage, it is important to highlight other perspectives on this matter by Western philosophers and sociologists. Amongst the older philosophers that studied this topic is Aristotle who believed that it is necessary for two members of any species, each in need of the other indispensably, to join together to reproduce. According to Aristotle, this is very natural because all living things have a natural desire to reproduce a successor reflecting itself. It is an innate desire for continuity. On the other hand, there are philosophers who have an opinion that the objective of marriage is to raise children and grant them wealth. Another school of thought promotes that there are various factors that motivate marriage such as economic security, a desire to have a home and fam-

---

[2] The Holy Quran. Chapter 56. [The Winnowing Winds; Arabic: *Al-Dhariyat*]. Verse 51.

ily, emotional security, attaining a particular social status, increasing wealth, and other advancements.

The common denominators between these various theories are the economic dimension and satisfaction of sexual desire. This is contrary to the Islamic understanding which views the relationship as one that comports with the innate nature that God has imparted in mankind. God describes this in the Holy Quran as a sign from amongst His signs, and a marker to His existence.

Islam embraces the relationship between man and woman as a natural phenomenon that conforms to mankind's innate nature. This relationship is a sign from amongst the signs of God. We ask, what is so particular and significant about marriage that elevates it to being a sign from amongst the signs of the Almighty? There are three factors that make it a divine sign.

Harmony, Affection, and Mercy

God created from every soul a companion for it. The source is the same for both but God divided it into male and female. Just as man needs and desires the woman physically and spiritually, the woman also needs and desires the man physically and spiritually. That is because they originate from one soul – each part desires the other to complete it.

God created the human with mixed feelings and emotions that occupy his intellect, heart, and soul. There needs to be something that calms and comforts these feelings and emotions. Marriage is the best means that leads to the stability and tranquility of the soul. God describes marriage with beautiful words such as 'dwelling' and 'stability'. The Prophet is famously known to have said, "Whoever gets married achieves half of his faith, so let him fear God in the other half."[3] A healthy marriage satisfies the needs of men and women, and their home becomes a dwelling for all their desires. So long as the proper foundation is there, a person's stability and comfort resides in their home with their spouse.

Islam considers marriage a sacred relationship that receives the highest level of respect because it is built on the harmony of souls. Marriage is not merely meant for physical intimacy that controls the fire of sexual desire; rather it is a relationship between two souls that produces love, affection, and mercy for humanity. It is the combination and balance between the physical, spiritual, emotional, and intellectual dimensions of a man and a woman that produces the most beautiful harmony, affection, and mercy. All of these dimensions must be considered and taken care of. If one is neglected, the others suffer.

THE BENEFITS OF MARRIAGE

After understanding the position of Islam on marriage, it is useful to examine some of the benefits and wisdoms behind it.

The Need for Intimacy

There is no doubt that sex is a powerful desire human beings experience throughout life. When such a basic desire is not fulfilled it often leads to feelings of instability, resorting

---

[3] Al-Kulayni, *Al-Kafi*, 5:329.

to bad alternatives, and other problems in mental health. Marriage is the best natural means to satisfy this desire. Through marriage, a person can satisfy his sexual needs and have that balance, happiness, and tranquility. He will be able to shield himself from falling into sin and violating people's rights. Otherwise, a person increases the likelihood of falling into sin and immoral alternatives that really bring nothing but more frustration and instability.

Raising a Family

One of the primary goals of marriage is to reproduce and continue the existence of mankind. Marriage is the best means for ensuring the continuity of humanity because it allows for the preservation of lineage. God gives great importance to the preservation of lineage because it contributes to the stability of communities. We find that communities that embrace the protection of lineage through promoting the proper mechanisms of reproduction are more stable than the communities that do not. Just think about the difference between a child that grows up in the comfort of two loving, righteous parents and one that is raised by one parent not knowing who the other parent is. The latter child will experience a huge void in his life and will naturally be disadvantaged by not having a mother or father. Both parents play a vital unique role, and the absence of one is detrimental to the overall growth and success of a child.

Psychological State

Most psychological qualities are acquired. They grow and develop in a person through nurture and experience. The desire of motherhood and fatherhood plays a massive role in developing certain qualities in a person such as love, mercy, and empathy. This desire or instinctual need does not develop and nurture in a person except through having children. When a person becomes a father or mother and raises children, he or she will view people and community around him or her with more compassion and mercy. Islam emphasized the importance of acquiring and developing these psychological qualities which can only be through marriage and having children.

One of the destructive qualities in a person is the ego. The more the ego flourishes in a person, the more oppressive and tyrannical he or she can become. Marriage and having children calms that ego. When a person is married and has children, they naturally assume a greater responsibility in taking care of others. Life no longer just revolves around them. Their concern and priority expands beyond themselves and that typically helps in curtailing the 'I' in them.

Economic State

As we have discussed, marriage compels one to feel a greater sense of responsibility than he or she would as an unmarried person. With marriage comes more financial obligations and commitment. This will motivate a person to struggle and work harder to provide for his family. That sense of motivation will lead a person to explore different ways to make a dignified living. Often times a person will become creative and innovative to discover new ways to make a living, all of which is positive for the economic prosperity of the community.

Social State

Marriage is a way for social bonding to take place between different families and communities. A stranger becomes a family member as is mentioned in the verse, "And He is who has created man from the water, then He has made for him blood relationship and marriage relationship, and your Lord is powerful."[4]

Stronger bonds between individuals in a community will reduce the social problems in that community. Consequently, we find that there are less social and moral problems in rural communities than urban communities because they tend to have closer knit families. Larger diverse communities are great, but they also run the risk of becoming spread apart and losing that closeness that is often the foundation that helps people stay morally strong and mentally awake.

Metaphysical State

What distinguishes a righteous Muslim from others is the belief in the metaphysical world and the ability of the Almighty. There are many acts that have a tangible impact but cannot be interpreted or explained, forcing one to concede to God's wisdom, knowledge, and power.

One such unexplainable phenomenon that is mentioned by the holy verses and prophetic traditions is the correlation between marriage and sustenance. Marriage is one of the acts that results in an increase in sustenance. God alludes to this in the Holy Quran where He says,

---

[4] The Holy Quran. Chapter 25. [The Criterion; Arabic: *Al-Furqaan*]. Verse 54.

*Marry those among you who are single, or the virtuous ones
among yourselves, male or female, if they are in poverty,
God will give them means out of His grace, for God is
Ample-Giving, Knowing.[5]*

Imam Al-Baqir also touches on this point by narrating on
behalf of the Holy Prophet, "Take on a family, for it will increase your sustenance."[6]

From experience, believers can testify that their sustenance
often increases in wondrous ways after they get married.
Many may think that getting married naturally would increase your financial burden, but somehow married people
often find that their financial opportunity is increased instead. Both the holy verse and the Prophet's words affirm
that marriage brings an increase in sustenance, which should
comfort the fear that some people have about the financial
burdens of marriage and raising a family. It is God's promise.

CONFORMING TO OUR PRINCIPLES

Islam has always adopted a consistent position in proactively encouraging marriage. It instituted laws and regulations
that simplify the process of marriage and attempt to remove
all obstacles that hinder it. Nonetheless, there remain hurdles and problems that obstruct the process of marriage in
addition to a host of cultural practices that violate Islamic
teachings. It is imperative to discuss two critical issues here:

---

[5] The Holy Quran. Chapter 24. [The Light; Arabic: *Al-Noor*]. Verse 32.
[6] Al-Sadouq *Man La Yahdaruh Al-Faqih*, 3:383.

1) the obstacles and problems, and 2) negative cultural traditions.

Obstacles and Problems

There are a number of obstacles and problems that we need to examine in order to figure out practical solutions.

Delayed Marriage. One of the major problems that young people face is the cultural expectation that marriage comes after a certain age – often around or after being 25 years old. For the male, he needs to graduate from school, start working, and establish himself so he can be financially capable to support a family. For the female, although financial capability is not a prerequisite for marriage, there is an expectation that she completes her education and launches her career. This results in a gap between the age of puberty and sexual maturity and the age of marriage.

Consider that a person has already gone through puberty in their early teen years for one. They have developed the emotional, psychological, and physical needs for intimacy with the opposite sex. Then they are told to wait about 10 to 15 years to fulfill those essential needs. If there is no available outlet for the young man or woman, a person might resort to the wrong alternatives to fulfill their desires – be it physical, emotional, or psychological. This is where you see the rise of dating, be it private or even public, and the epidemic of pornography and masturbation. Young people have resorted to these outlets because the hope of getting married at a young age is often shunned by their surrounding culture and the expectations around them. This problem is rising on a daily basis in our communities as it has been increasingly difficult for young people to establish themselves and become financially capable to pursue marriage.

We have to realize that every action a person engages in will leave an impact on his or her soul. If his actions deviate from the course God prescribed, the effect will be detrimental on the person individually and consequently, on the community at large because the community is made up of its individuals. The negative effects of delayed marriage on the community include, but are not limited to, the following:

1. Moral deviation by adopting new customs and habits including dating and masturbation.
2. The rise of mental health issues associating with not fulfilling one's sexual desires, or fulfilling it through improper alternatives such as masturbation and fornication.
3. The increase in aversion to marriage, which is more common in non-Islamic communities. This aversion is a product of the normalization of unlawful relationships in mainstream society.
4. A lack of reliance on God and adopting more materialistic worldviews on marriage and society by having the predominant focus of communion being financially driven.

There is no doubt that Islam is the religion of the innate – meaning that religion is a host of ethical laws and concepts that are compatible with our human nature. Thus, we will not find any discrepancy or conflict between the innate that God has created in us and what He prescribed to guide our decisions and actions. God has blessed both males and females with the ability to come together and marry. Furthermore, through the prophetic traditions, God promotes early marriage.

We must be reminded that God knows us best because He created us. He knows what is in our best interest. He knows our circumstances. He knows our abilities. We must have faith that what He instructs and encourages us to do is best for us. Consequently, Islam views early marriage as the best option for mankind. However, we create many social hurdles and obstacles that can obstruct early marriage. Islam teaches us to remove these hurdles and obstacles, because if we do not there will be consequences that can compromise the health and wellbeing of our communities.

Some communities have normalized unlawful relations between men and women to the extent that sex outside of marriage is no longer frowned upon. When sexual engagement does not have any bounds then people are not protected. Their rights are not observed and the dignity of the individual is not respected. Marriage protects both a man and a woman's rights. It makes both parties aware of their responsibilities towards one another, and more so it does not allow one side to take advantage of the other as what is often seen in relationships outside of marriage. Marriage is a commitment that both parties have to observe. Again, Islam does not take a person's respect and dignity lightly. The sanctity of an individual is one of the greatest and most revered things on God's earth. Through marriage, that sanctity is preserved and respect is protected. Islam attempts to counter the proliferation of relationships outside of marriage by advocating for early marriage. It is narrated that the Holy Prophet said,

> O youth, whoever amongst you can get married should get married, for marriage protects the sight and shields the private parts. Whoever cannot pursue marriage should fast routinely because fasting is a protection and safeguard.[7]

The Benefits of Early Marriage. There are a number of important benefits to early marriage that we should pay attention to. Socially, there are numerous gains. First, when a person's sexual desires are satisfied, he will be more mentally and physically stable. This will result in a rise of productivity because a person will be able to think and act more effectively. On the contrary, if a person is consistently struggling with his sexual desire, he will be consumed and distracted mentally and physically.

Second, if a couple marry at a younger age, they will be more flexible to change their habits to reach a mutual state of compatibility. It becomes increasingly difficult for one that is older to amend his habits and customs. Younger couples will naturally be more flexible to accommodate one another by dropping negative habits and developing positive ones. This flexibility will contribute to a more stable marriage and family. Another social upside to early marriage is that it is more likely that younger couples will have a better support system from their parents and families.

Finally, in the case that a young married woman lives with her in-laws, at least in the early years of marriage, it will help her create a stronger and more intimate bond with his fami-

---

[7] Al-Tabrasi, *Makarim Al-Akhlaq*, 197.

ly members. Moreover, in this case where the young couple lives with the husband's family, the couple will benefit financially because their expenses will be substantially less than if they were to live on their own. This will afford them the opportunity to work, save money, and be able to afford to live independently in their near future.

Early marriage will also help the couple with raising their children. It becomes increasingly challenging for parents to have and raise children as they get older. It is more manageable for a 25-year-old parent to carry the burden of raising a child than a 40 or 50-year-old parent. One of the reasons why is because younger parents will have less of a gap between them and their kids, which will allow them to better understand and connect with them. Younger parents are more likely to bridge the age and cultural gap with their children, understand their times and circumstances, and connect with them more effectively.

The Rise in Dowry and Marriage Expenses. One of the major impediments that obstructs a successful marriage built on faith is the rising expense of dowry. This is a serious issue that needs to be addressed.

The economic and financial growth in modern society has contributed to the unprecedented rise of dowries. This exponential rise in dowries has become a tax on marriage that made it all the more difficult for young men to pursue marriage. It deters young men from wanting to get married because they are discouraged by the financial burden that has come before even getting married and living with his new spouse.

One of the reasons behind the rise in dowries is the increase in marital requirements by the bride, including clothes, jewelry, accessories, and other popular expenses. The economic advancement in society compels women to dress and look in a certain way. The bride's parents place this burden on the groom. Thus, they increase their demands to meet what they view as necessary for their daughter.

Other people view dowry as a form of insurance for the wife, especially with the escalation of divorce. Some families believe that a substantial dowry payment will force the man to think twice before considering divorce or a second marriage. They also view the dowry as an insurance policy that will assist the wife if she ends up divorced and on her own.

Some communities associate the amount of the dowry with the value of the bride. In other words, they view a higher dowry as showing more value and worth for the bride. This also creates a sense of negative and unhealthy competition between families. Some families put a hefty price tag on their daughters to show a false and superficial sense of value and self-worth.

This is utter ignorance and nonsense. The dowry must not be a price tag on the daughter nor a competition between families. However, some people live their whole life relentless to outcompete others in every way possible. For them, this is just another battle and competition. In the end, all of this is rooted in ignorance, discontent, and the attempt by some to appear wealthy when in fact they might not be.

The issue of expensive dowries is not novel in Islam. It has transcended time and nations. Islam remained steadfast and firm against this prevailing phenomenon, in theory and in practice.

In theory, there are countless traditions that resent pricey dowries and advocate for a discounted dowry. One narration mentions that the blessings of a woman are in the scarcity of her dowry, and her misfortune is in the abundance of her dowry.[8]

This matter was implemented by practice through the Prophet's family. When Imam Ali married Lady Fatima, the Prophet's beloved daughter, the Holy Prophet requested a humble dowry on her behalf – 500 dirhams[9]. The dowry did not translate to how he valued his daughter. No material thing could encapsulate the value of the greatest woman to walk this earth, nor how God's Prophet valued his beloved daughter.

What the Prophet did here was set an example for all of us. He showed us that the dowry of marriage does not determine the value of the individual, nor is it meant to be an insurance policy to deter divorce or take care of the woman in case divorce is the result. The dowry of Lady Fatima, 500 dirhams or what is today valued at about $850, is the recommended amount for a bride's dowry following the tradition of the Holy Prophet. Although Lady Zahra's dowry is nominal, it transcended time and became a long-time tradition for the believers.

---

[8] Al-Sadouq, *Man La Yahdaruh Al-Faqih*, 3:387

[9] A dirham is a silver coin historically used as currency. Each dirham was minted using approximately 3 grams of silver. The dinar was also used. The dinar is a gold currency used in early Islamic times. At the time, each dinar was made of a "mithqal" (about 4.25 to 4.5 grams) of gold.

It is imperative to not lose sight of the true purpose of a dowry. In Islam, a dowry is to be utilized to prepare the house for the bride, which is what the Prophet did with Lady Fatima's dowry. He utilized most of the money to purchase furniture for her home and used the remaining amount for a dinner in honor of the marriage.

Islam does not obligate the woman to use her dowry to furnish her home. However, this is the example the Prophet set for us and we should emulate it. The dowry is a monetary gift for the wife to furnish her home and purchase essential needs that are consistent with her taste. It is in fact a tool to purchase the essentials necessary to build a home.

There is a serious implication in associating the value of the dowry with the value of the bride. We are essentially putting a price tag on the bride. We are doing a great disservice to her as a sacred human being by treating her like any other product in the market to be sold and bought. This surely has a negative psychological impact on the bride, as well as on the culture of the community.

During irreparable conflicts between the spouses, God has prescribed divorce. However, in the case where the husband paid a pricey dowry, he will be less inclined to divorce. They may both want the divorce, but because of the dowry he will hold out and the relationship would only get uglier. In worse scenarios, he might request a repayment of the dowry as a condition for divorce. This will add to the rift between the couple and escalate the conflict, all of which is to the detriment of all parties involved.

We find solutions to all of our problems in our Islamic traditions. Collectively, we must accept the idea of reducing the dowries in marriage and adhere to the example that the Prophet established. A marriage that is built following the example of Lady Fatima will gain God's favor and grace.

It is not absurd that a wealthy businessman would request a high dowry for his daughter given his social status. However, if he would decide to break the expected trend he would earn people's respect and admiration. When the wealthy in the community make a conscious effort to change the expectation on dowries, they will be easing the path of the young men in the community towards marriage that is void of emphasis on the material things in life. That in turn will bring blessings to their daughters and be an excellent foundation for happy and successful marriages.

What great honor for a righteous young lady to stand on Judgement Day before Lady Fatima, knowing that she followed in her footsteps. It could be this very act that can intercede for a woman on that great day. Thus, our daughters should also be conscious and take position not to be treated as a product with a price tag.

As such the Islamic dowry established by the Prophet is the real value for the woman, not monetarily but rather morally. A wife should be cognizant that a dowry is never a true insurance for her nor is it a reflection of her value. If she is happy and satisfied with her husband, then everything he owns is for her and her children. And if she is unhappy and dissatisfied with her husband, then all of the money in the world will not bring her happiness or alleviate her misery.

Finally, our sisters and daughters should be aware that overburdening the husband financially can truly detriment the marriage short term and long term. What good do lofty dowries, expensive gifts, and extravagant homes do when the husband becomes drowned in debt and a prisoner to banks? This will lead to tension, resentment, and misery in the home, all of which can compromise the relationship and risk bringing it to a bitter end.

Social Compatibility Between Spouses. One of the major problems that obstructs marriages is the compatibility in terms of social status between spouses. Although this issue has deep historical roots, it has become more prevalent in modern days due to a number of reasons.

First, the rise of diversity in our contemporary societies and the presence of many ethnicities in one community has created further comparison and issues of superiority between families and groups. Every group or ethnicity believes it is superior to others. This sometimes creates a culture where a couple from two different ethnicities are viewed as unequal in status.

Second, with the growing economic disparity in our communities, wealthy families sometimes feel a sense of superiority over those less endowed. Such families will only allow their sons or daughters to marry from families that share the same financial status. Otherwise, they will reject a spouse from a family that financially inferior or that does not have a similar socioeconomic status.

Third, education has increasingly become a major factor in determining social compatibility. A young man typically desires to marry a well-educated graduate. Inversely, a young woman will also demand a husband that is educated and has a reputable degree. If either is lacking, families are quick to judge negatively on the young man or woman.

Fourth, career disparity has also contributed to the problem of social incompatibility between spouses. This is more particular to women who lead successful careers. Some of these women who are financially independent will expect to marry someone who is either equal or superior to them in terms of career and earnings. Take the example of a female physician who is established in her career and makes an impressive salary. Even if her future husband is an architect or engineer, respected in his industry, but does not earn as much as she does, she will not consider him. These are some of the reasons that have contributed to the rise and growth of this social phenomena, which has resulted in serious social problems.

Social compatibility has always been an issue in Islamic communities. During the Prophet's time, it was ubiquitous considering the strong presence of tribalism amongst the Arabs. Islam came and addressed social compatibility head on through the Prophet's teachings and examples.

Amongst the many examples the Prophet set was with the marriage of Duba'a Bint Zubair Ibn Abdulmuttalib. Imam Al-Sadiq narrates,

> The Messenger of God married Al-Muqdad Ibn Al-Aswad to Duba'a Bint Zubair Ibn Abdulmuttalib... He married her to Al-Muqdad so that [social class should not be the determinant of marriage] and that you can emulate the Prophet, and so that you know that the most honorable of you in the sight of God is the most righteous...[10]

---

[10] Al-Kulayni, *Al-Kafi*, 5:344.

Another example the Prophet set was with the marriage of Juwaiber. Imam Al-Baqir narrated his story. One day, Juwaiber came to the Prophet desiring to enter Islam. He became a good Muslim. Juwaiber was living a very rough life. He was unattractive, poor, and did not have family. The Prophet took him under his wing. He gave him food, clothing, and a home.

At some point the Prophet looked at Juwaiber and encouraged him to get married. Juwaiber told the Prophet that no woman would accept him as a husband. He did not have money to support a new household, a family to lean on, nor the looks and charm at the least. The Prophet assured Juwaiber that Islam came to embrace all people and that the only standard is the piety of a person.

The Prophet took it upon himself to get Juwaiber married, and he made it happen. Not only did Juwaiber marry, but he married a young lady from a prominent family despite the initial opposition from the bride's father. The Prophet used this example to break all artificial social standards that people created in assessing a candidate for marriage. It did not matter how wealthy you were, what family you belonged to, or how physically attractive you were. What mattered was your character, your faith, your virtue and ethics.

Islam's measure for compatibility is faith. A righteous bride is compatible with a righteous groom, although they might have disparities in family, wealth, and social status. The Prophet proclaimed clearly that the true standard for compatibility is faith. He said, "If someone comes [i.e. to propose for marriage] who you are satisfied with his morals and faith, marry him. If you do not, there will be sedition and corruption on earth."[11]

As to financial compatibility, it is critical to remember it is important but sustenance is truly in the hands of God. How many people were wealthy and then became poor and how many people were poor but then became wealthy? The distribution of wealth is controlled by God. Our job is to strive and work hard, but leave the rest to God. Marriage is no exception. When we probe into some communities that are more materialistically driven, we find that sometimes marriage becomes like a commercial deal between two companies – the families. We also find that some do not desire to marry their daughters to outsiders because they fear that their wealth will go to strangers.

If we assume that a person's money goes to his daughter after his demise, isn't this money essentially going to his grandchildren? So what if the daughter spends the money on her children. Isn't a father's ultimate goal to see his daughter and her family happy? If a father approves a righteous man for his daughter, wouldn't he be assured that the husband will never lay a finger on his daughter? What good is money if it cannot create happiness or if it becomes a source of misery for the family?

With regards to men Imam Al-Sadiq narrates, "If a man marries a woman for her looks or wealth, that is all he will get. However, if he marries her for her faith, God will bless him with money and beauty."[12] Islam once again reiterates

---

[11] Al-Tousi, *Al-Amaali*, 519.
[12] Al-Kulayni, *Al-Kafi*, 5:333.

that the standard for social compatibility is not financial status, but rather faith and piety.

Finally, as it pertains to the educational and career compatibility, the nature of the problem is similar to that of social and financial compatibility. Education and career is not the Islamic standard for measuring compatibility. The real wealth that ought to be assessed in a person is his knowledge, manners, and piety. As is the case with money, knowledge is useless if it is not used in the way of God. If people continue to use the wrong metrics to assess the compatibility of a person, we will be perpetuating what the Prophet describes as "sedition and corruption on earth." Let us follow the impeccable examples the Ahlulbayt set for us by applying the right standards for evaluating a prospective spouse for our daughters and sons, and dismiss once and for all the artificial and arbitrary standards burdening our families.

What Happens at Weddings?

The wedding is an important milestone in a person's life. It is a significant event not only for the bride and groom, but also for their families and community. However, we find the presence of numerous wrong customs and traditions associated with weddings in various cultures. Many weddings unfortunately have become a source of unnecessary extravagance and falling to sin.

The Unnecessary Extravagance. It has become the norm for marriage to be a display of imprudent and wasteful spending by the two parties involved and their guests. Yes, the wedding ceremony is a once in a lifetime occasion and the bride desires to look in the best appearance possible.

However, that does not justify for one to disobey God by engaging in the impermissible, especially with extravagant expenditures.

Islam promotes generosity in hosting guests to honor the union of bride and groom. It is recommended to host a feast during the wedding of the new couple. It is narrated that Imam Al-Ridha said,

> *When the Prophet married Um Habiba Amina Bint Abu Sufyan, he hosted a feast and said, 'One of the prophetic traditions is to feed [guests] during marriage [i.e. wedding].*[13]

It is recommended to host a feast during five specific occasions: after a child is born, circumcision, purchasing a home, returning from the hajj pilgrimage, and marriage. Our communities have consistently embraced hosting a feast during marriage, which is commendable. However, the problem with some of these feasts is the fact that they have become a show for extravagance and waste. Lavish dinners in extravagant restaurants and hotels are not a reflection of virture and happiness; they are merely superficial – a façade. Or when so much food is prepared and the bulk of it ends up in the trash, what does that reflect? Is that a way to honor God's favor upon us or is it not a blatant disregard for His blessings? We have to be mindful that there are many needy families that sleep on empty stomachs. Instead of disposing of excessive food, it should be passed out to hungry families that are in dire need of our help. All of this goes back to mindfulness and being conscious of what we do. If we do

---

[13] Al-Barqi, *Al-Mahasen*, 2:418.

not have our priorities straight, decide to be selfish and inconsiderate, then we are going to be making the wrong choices and fall further into sin.

Falling to Sin. One of the worst aspects that come along with weddings is the extent that sin is overlooked. From music and dancing to immodesty and extravagance, it is all too prevalent. We need to take a step back and examine the rise of this unfortunate trend in our communities. It is disheartening to find such good families, who are even considered to be "religious" within their community, to be accepting of such acts when it comes to wedding. The excuse is, "It's only one day." But our faith is not reserved for some days and excused on others. Islam is a way of life and should be honored and respected every day of our lives.

A person who identifies with the school of Ahlulbayt should strictly adhere to their teachings and instructions-both in words and actions. Imam Al-Sadiq alludes to this in a famous narration where he states, "Be an adornment for us, not a disgrace."[14]

A believer should be an example for others to follow. As followers of Ahlulbayt it is unbecoming of us to be found in the center of music and dancing at weddings. Imam Ali captured this when he told his followers, "Good from anyone is good but from you it is better, due to your status from us [i.e. Ahlulbayt]. And what is bad from anyone is bad but from you it is worse."[15] As proud followers of the Imam, we should manifest the principles and values of Ahlulbayt in everything we do.

---

14 Al-Majlisi, *Bihar Al-Anwar*, 75:348.

15 Ibn Shahrashoob, *Al-Manaqib*, 3:362.

It is vital for a wise person, whether he considers himself to be religious or not, to be calculative about this matter. Is it better for one to spend money and put on an impermissible show with music and dancing just to conform to a misguided norm or leverage the wedding as an opportunity to bring families and the greater community together? If people are not willing to abolish music in weddings for religious purposes, let them do it for the sake of being encompassing and inclusive for family and friends that would not attend otherwise.

Marriage is a sacred union that is glorified and honored by God. This institution is only built with the remembrance of the Almighty. It should be observed as such. Is it not paradoxical that we would begin in God's name but end the night with a party characteristic of music, dancing, and heedlessness? Imam Al-Sadiq said, "A house [characteristic] of music will not be safe from the infliction of tragedies… supplications will not be answered in it, and the angels will not enter it."[16]

The decision to employ music and impermissible entertainment in a wedding at the outset of marriage has serious ramifications. It is a significant decision that will shape the course of the marriage from the outset. On that night, the married couple will be either seeking God and inviting his blessings and mercy or disobeying Him and rejecting his bounties. The real effects of these sins, like many others, may not be felt immediately or in the short-term. The effects can be long-term and they can implicate their children and grandchildren. Therefore, a person should think twice

---

[16] Al-Kulayni, Al-Kafi, 6:433.

before falling to these sins; if not concerned for himself he should be concerned for his progeny.

Every community's originality and authenticity can be assessed by its adherence to its traditions and customs. A community that does not have a rich history lacks originality. When we examine the traditions associated with weddings in our Islamic culture, we find pleasant and beautiful traditions that are connected to our history and faith. For example, it is common to recite the story of the Prophet's marriage and moving poetry about the Prophet and the Imams. These practices show a deeply rooted bond between the community and the religious teachings and principles. With that said, it is truly disheartening to replace these rich traditions with negative practices, such as music and dancing, that contradict the spirit of Islam with superficial means of celebration.

It is strange and baffling at the same time to notice some of the contradictions we have in our society. Our society is generally known to be conservative and modest. Although there are reservations pertaining to how some women wear the Hijab – as some seem to be more concerned about looking fashionable than modest – it is safe to say that our communities appreciate modesty and make an effort to be conscious of problematic environments. Nonetheless, this awareness seems to evaporate during weddings. Unfortunately, some men accept for their wives, daughters, and relatives to be exposed in inappropriate ways during these events, compromising the modesty that we hold dear as a religious community. We should not turn a blind eye to these things. The change begins on an individual level. We all have to take responsibility, reflect, and make the necessary steps towards what is best.

WOMEN IN ISLAM

In the name of God, the most Beneficent, the most Merciful

God draws another example for those who have faith: the wife of Pharaoh, when she said, 'My Lord! Build me a home near You in paradise, and deliver me from Pharaoh and his conduct, and deliver me from the wrongdoing lot.'[1]

Women manifest the continuity and proliferation of the human being. Through women comes life. Through women there is life. The progeny of Adam could only come with the existence of Eve. That was God's will. From Adam and Eve there would be scores of women that would not only birth the noblest of men but also be themselves noble, virtuous, and godly saints to whom the whole world would look up to. Asia[2], the wife of Pharaoh, was such a woman. Her commitment to God was unmatched. Her resilience and perseverance could be compared to none of her time, especially given the circumstances in which she lived. The wife of a tyrant, but nonetheless one of the noblest women

---

[1] The Holy Quran. Chapter 66. [The Forbidding; Arabic: *Al-Tahreem*]. Verse 11.

[2] Asia bint Muzahem was the wife of the Pharaoh who reigned at the time of Prophet Moses. She is revered as one of the greatest women of all time, along with Lady Mariam, Lady Khadija, and Lady Fatima. – Eds.

to walk God's earth. She protected Moses and allowed for his message to reign throughout Egypt. She went against all the odds and placed her trust in God alone. She was that example of excellence that humanity strives to emulate. Islam propagates her example, and the example of all women who followed in her footsteps. A woman's example is not merely for women of course, it is for men and women alike. We see that Islam's perspective of women is no less than that of man, and could never be compared as such. Unfortunately, there does exist a bad misconception about Islam's view on women. This misconception, like many others, is often due to the actions and choices of individuals rather than the system of belief itself.

People often attribute things to the faith as a reflection of the practices of Muslims. So if a Muslim abuses a woman, then it must be because Islam condones such abuse. If a Muslim carries out an act of violence against a person of another faith, it must be because Islam promotes crimes against humanity. Though there are some Muslims that deal with women in an abusive, violent, repulsive manner – ways that certainly do not reflect the teachings of Islam – it does not mean that Islam tolerates such behavior. The oppression of women that exists in some societies, be it through physical abuse, social suppression, or other forms of injustice, is often due to other backgrounds associated with some Muslims' identities. Looking particularly at the Middle East or the Arab World, you will find that these practices are a continuation of the customs and traditions that existed during the pre-Islamic era of *Jahiliya* – also known as the Age of Ignorance.

During this time, women were looked at with contempt. Like in many other parts of the world, women were treated as second-class citizens. They were considered to be inferior to men and only in existence to serve the whims of their male counterparts. This backwards and distorted understanding took women as mere instruments. It was this very outlook that Islam came to do away with, given its harmful impact on society and the injustice it permeated throughout families and communities. The Holy Prophet's message enfranchised women and disentangled the barriers that women faced in society. We see this with the way he brought up his own home and what examples he set through his own family. One of the greatest examples of that came through his wife Khadija bint Khuwaylid.

Lady Khadija was the first Muslim to accept the Prophet's message. Yes, a woman was the first and foremost adherent to the final religion of God. She wasn't any woman for that matter. Khadija was a merchant, a businesswoman, something almost unheard of for women during her time. Not only was she a businesswoman, but she owned and operated one of the most successful enterprises in Arabia. Dozens if not hundreds of employees and agents worked for her business established and traveled lands near and far under her flagship. In fact, Prophet Muhammad actually worked as a merchant for a period of time in her enterprise. The Prophet would go on to marry Khadija and from that marriage would come the pride and joy of the Prophet, his daughter Fatima. Lady Fatima's status was so sacred, even though she would only live until the age of eighteen, that she would join the ranks of her mother Khadija, Mary[3] the mother of Jesus, and Asia the wife of the Pharaoh – the Greatest of Women.

Nonetheless, there are Muslims that practice certain things that are mistakenly taken as a reflection of Islam's teachings, when in reality there are not. Some have misinterpreted or misapplied the notion of *Qaymouma* – which is understood as the authority of men over women. When people look at authority they often mistaken it for ownership, mastership, or some sort of dictator to subject relationship. This is way off from the original principal. Husbands and fathers are generally tasked with guardianship over their families, which includes their wives and children. They have a responsibility, a duty, to take care of their families and provide for them. Men are responsible for the wellbeing, safety, and overall health of their families. They are not empowered to be oppressive to their women; rather, they are obligated to be kind and caring, generous and giving, and responsible and mindful.

ISLAM AND WOMEN

Islam repeatedly emphasizes the great status that women enjoy in the eyes of God. This is evident when we look at what Islam offers women and the transformation it has led to change the way women are perceived in society, specifically after the Age of Ignorance with the advent of the Prophet's message.

---

[3] Mary or Mariam bint Imran was the daughter of Prophet Imran and the mother of Prophet Jesus. She is regarded as one of greatest women of all time along with Lady Asia, Lady Khadija, and Lady Fatima. – Eds.

In the Holy Quran and the Noble Narrations

God does not speak to men exclusively in the Holy Quran, nor did the Holy Prophet do so in his directives with people. The conversation always encompassed men and women alike. Divine commandments came to humanity. The verses of the Holy Quran, speaking to the believers or humanity at large, address both men and women equally. Furthermore, the obligations imposed by God are incumbent on both sexes. There is no preferential treatment given to men over women, nor women over men. Take a look at the following verse in which God stresses the same attributes for both men and women.

> *Indeed the Muslim men and the Muslim women, the faithful men and the faithful women, the obedient men and the obedient women, the truthful men and the truthful women, the patient men and the patient women, the humble men and the humble women, the charitable men and the charitable women, the men who fast and the women who fast, the men who guard their private parts and the women who guard, the men who remember God greatly and the women who remember [God greatly] —God holds in store for them forgiveness and a great reward.[4]*

This Quranic verse reinforces the attributes of a perfect human being – obedience, patience, devotion, chastity, and piety. Again, these attributes are meant for both male and female, addressing them on the same very level. In adhering to these principles, the reward is God's blessings, forgiveness and grace.

---

[4] The Holy Quran. Chapter 33. [The Confederates; Arabic: *Al-Ahzab*]. Verse 35.

In the same light, God speaks of the comradery of the faithful, both men and women, in promoting a sense of brotherhood and sisterhood amongst believers. It is not that one merely believes in God and emulates those divine attributes, but believers help one another to reach that great status with God.

> But the faithful, men and women, are comrades of one another: they bid what is right and forbid what is wrong and maintain the prayer, give the zakat, and obey God and His Apostle. It is they to whom God will soon grant His mercy. Indeed God is all-mighty, all-wise.[5]

The Prophet did not differentiate between men and women in his dealings, especially with respect to important matters of the state. In relation to the matter of allegiance, the Prophet would have men and women be involved in the same way. Before he departed this world, he assigned Imam Ali as his successor – leader and guardian over the people's affairs – by divine order. Men and women, alike, would pay allegiance to Imam Ali after the Prophet made the public announcement of succession at Ghadeer Khum.[6] By the Prophet's order, women were engaged in public affairs. Their voice and allegiance was held in the same regard as men, and thus you saw their participation as such and the Prophet's emphasis on their representation.

The attention given to women in the Holy Quran is quite apparent. God speaks of the noblest of women as exem-

---

[5] The Holy Quran. Chapter 9. [Repentance; Arabic: *Al-Tawbah*]. Verse 71.

[6] The announcement took place after the Prophet's Farewell Pilgrimage, in the last year of his life, in a place known as Ghadeer Khum between Mecca and Medina. – Eds.

plars of truth, justice, honor, and wisdom. Many verses speak of the pure saint Lady Mary. Beyond being the mother of one of the greatest of God's prophets and messengers, Mary was honored by God for her unwavering faith, unshakeable piety, and her crystal purity. In addition to Lady Mary, you will find a number of verses in reference to Lady Asia, like the one at the very beginning of this chapter. God made her an exemplar not only for women, but for all believers throughout time. She abandoned the life of royalty and luxury because she put God and her faith first. Asia endured unimaginable torture for the sake of her creed. She was without a doubt one of the best people to walk God's earth.

Lady Khadija and Lady Fatima would come with the story of Prophet Muhammad, both characterized by a life of sacrifice and generosity. No one would be turned away from their doors. After Lady Khadija passed away, the young Fatima would take care of her father despite her youth. There are plenty of traditions that describe her virtues and status in the eyes of God and His Prophet. For one, the Prophet referred to her as the "Mother of her Father," given the motherly care and affection she provided him. Of course, the Prophet did not speak in vain nor out of his own whim. And even if his words came in part due to his affection for his daughter as a loving father, his words were always a reflection of God's revelation. As God says, "He does not speak out of whim, he is nothing but revelation."[7]

---

[7] The Holy Quran 53:3 – 4

God Honors Us All

When an individual is deprived of something, that does not mean that God is giving them less value or holds them in a lesser esteem. To the contrary, with God everything is created with purpose and nothing goes in vain. Some may assume that because women are not appointed for certain positions of leadership that they are lesser than men. For example, there are no prophets or messengers of God that are women. There is divine wisdom in that. Just like there is divine wisdom in having women be the sole source from which prophets are born, cared for and brought up. Men cannot give birth to children, nor can they provide the care of a mother. Again there is divine wisdom in that. The lack of women prophets or messengers is not because women are incapable of holding positions of leadership in society. You have the examples of Asia, Mary, Khadija, and Fatima to show otherwise.

The wisdom here is that God has given people roles and responsibilities. Though positions of governance and leadership have often been reserved for men, it is women who lead from the background and offer the source of inspiration, and existence for that matter, to proliferate for such leadership. Without women there are no men. Therefore, the philosophy pertaining to this can be understood as one that is concerned with role distribution. We probably cannot favor between the just governor, judicious adjudicator, and martyr in the way of God. The person who performs his duty in this life, in obedience to God, will win His satisfaction in any field in life. It can be the merchant who is sincere in his work to God, the scholar who is loyal in his work to God, the artisan who is faithful in his work to God, or the worker who is honest in his work to God. They are all equal. What is most important in Islam is honesty. A simple hardworking farmer who fulfills his role in this life and obeys God with sincerity is far better than an educated executive who cheats and scams people to get ahead for his own personal gain.

There is a pleasant anecdote from the life of the Holy Prophet regarding perceptions of roles and the rewards that come with them. The following narration speaks of a woman who went to the Holy Prophet to complain about a few things that had been on her mind, as well as the minds of her friends. Her name was Asmaa bint Yazeed Al-Ansaria. She came up to the Holy Prophet as he sat with some of his companions and said

> *May my father and mother be sacrificed for you. I have come to you as a delegate from the believing women. I know that there is no woman, in the East or West, that would have listened to what I have said and will not share my opinion. God has sent you as the truth for men and women, so we have believed in you and in your Lord that sent you. We women are confined and limited to our homes, satisfying men's pleasures, and carrying their children. Men have been favored by God over us with Fridays [i.e. by performing Friday prayers] and social gatherings, visiting the sick, and participating in funerals… If they go out on a mission, we protect their money, sow their clothes, and raise their children. Do we not have a share in the good deeds with you O' Messenger of God?*

After listening intently to the woman's plea, the Holy Prophet turned towards his companions and asked, "Have you heard better words from a woman inquiring about her faith than this?" All pleasantly surprised, they replied that they had not. The Prophet turned back to the woman and said,

> *Go, O' Asmaa, and inform the women with you that a woman who is a good spouse to her husband, seeks his contentment, and adheres to his acceptance, is equal to all of the acts of men that you have mentioned.*

Upon hearing the Prophet's response, she was filled with joy. She left the Prophet's company cheering the words, "God is Great! God is Great!"[8] The Prophet had assured her that though it may seem that her role is less significant when compared to the public responsibilities and activities that were custom of men; she should know that just her fulfilling her responsibility as a good wife was equal to all of that put together.

God states in the Holy Quran,

> *Then their Lord answered them, 'I do not waste the work of any worker among you, whether male or female; you are all on the same footing. So those who migrated and were expelled from their homes, and were tormented in My way, and those who fought and were killed – I will surely absolve them of their misdeeds and I will admit them into gardens*

---

8 Al-Reyshahri, *Mizan Al-Hikma*, 4:2869. Citing: Al-Siyouti, *Al-Dur Al-Manthur*, 2:152-153.

*with streams running in them, as a reward from God, and
with God is the best of rewards.*[9]

"You are all on the same footing," God tells us. There is no
superiority when it comes to the sexes. Each is unique and
is rewarded for their deeds and commitment to God's principles. Islam views the role of women as grand and nothing
short of the man's role, if not exceeding it in many situations. Women have often been the proponents behind the
triumph of truth. Their commitment to the word of God
through their faith, piety, and intellect has preserved and
protected God's religion and His people. We have beautiful
examples that were portrayed by some of the righteous
women in the everlasting divine tragedy of Karbala. This
tragedy implanted and rooted the teachings of Islam. God
willed to grant women their blessed role during this saga so
that they become an equal contributor with men. It suffices
that the success of Imam Hussain's renaissance was contingent on the role of his sister Lady Zainab. She was the
mouthpiece of his movement and propagator of his message. She told the tale of his tragedy and the massacre that
befell him and his companions. Through her advocacy and
rhetoric, she exposed Umayyad oppression just as her
brother Imam Hussain exposed them with the sacrifice of
his pure blood. That pure blood with her courageous advocacy were woven together to form an immaculate quilt for
Imam Hussain's blessed renaissance.

---

[9] The Holy Quran. Chapter 3. [The Family of Imran; Arabic: *Al-Imran*]. Verse
195.

HUSBAND & WIFE

In the name of God, the most Beneficent, the most Merciful

And of His signs is that He created for you mates from your own selves that you may take comfort in them, and He ordained affection and mercy between you. There are indeed signs in that for a people who reflect.[1]

It is no exaggeration to say that Islam did not give more attention to any matter than it did with the issue of family and marriage. That is because the family is the first building block in a community. If this building block or foundation is proper and solid, it will strengthen society as a whole. Contrastingly, if it is weak the building of society will be prone to collapse given its lacking foundation. The Prophet said, "There is nothing built in Islam more desirable and dear to God than marriage."[2] The Prophet is also narrated to have stated, "Whoever wants to meet God pure and purified, should meet Him with a spouse."[3]

---

[1] The Holy Quran. Chapter 30. [The Byzantines; Arabic: *Al-Rum*]. Verse 21.

[2] Al-Majlisi, *Bihar Al-Anwar*, 100:222.

[3] Ibid.

Islam has a comprehensive vision for marriage, as it has with all matters and aspects of life. For brevity's sake, we will shed some light on the marital rights and obligations between a husband and wife that are vital for the success of their marriage.

THE RIGHTS OF A WIFE

In his work, the Treatise on Rights, Imam Ali Al-Sajjad goes through a number of rights and obligations that we must observe. He includes the rights of parents, siblings, teachers, scholars, partners, companions, amongst many others. Of those mentioned the Imam discusses the rights of a wife.

> The right of your wife is that you know that God has made her a repose and a comfort for you; you should know that she is God's favor toward you, so you should honor her and treat her gently. Even when her right toward you is more incumbent, you must treat her with mercy...[4]

The existence of rights and obligations in a marriage are necessary for the marriage to be built on justice and equity. When those rights and obligations are not observed, it is natural for problems and conflicts to ensue between the couple. Islam, through its emphasis on outlining the rights and obligations in many of the social relationships, attempts to alleviate potential conflicts that can arise and ensure the protection of everyone's rights in a dispute.

We find that Islam puts special emphasis on being benevolent and compassionate and not limiting oneself to the established parameters and regulations, which aim to prevent

---

[4] Al-Majlisi, *Bihar Al-Anwar*, 71:5

authoritarianism and dispute. However, it is benevolence, charity, and altruism that should dictate our relationships.

The beauty of life does not radiate unless these principles prevail. Thus, it is imperative to understand that one should not limit himself to fulfilling these prescribed rights and obligations. These are only a minimum and anything more will be a form of benevolence and compassion that God commanded us to have in our social relationships generally, let alone in the most intimate bond which is between the husband and wife.

Based on that premise, let us discuss the rights of women first because of the regard Islam gave women generally. Women are the foundation of humanity's mercy, compassion, and affection. Thus, it is only natural that we should give women more consideration and appreciate their presence. Even when it comes to gift-giving, we often see a natural tendency to favor girls in priority over their brothers. It is like the Prophet said,

> *Whoever enters the market and purchases a masterpiece, and carries it to his dependents, is like the one who carries charity to a tribe of needy people. He should commence with the females before the males...*[5]

Women come before men given their respect as mothers and the birthers of life. Imam Al-Baqir speaks of the conversation between Prophet Moses and God on the significance of mothers.

> *Moses said, 'O God, advise me.'*
> *God said, 'I advise you of Me.'*

---

[5] Al-Majlisi, *Bihar Al-Anwar*, 110:69-94.

Moses said, 'God, advise me.'
God said, 'I advise you of Me' and repeated it three times.
Moses said, 'God advise me.'
God said, 'I advise you of your mother.'
Moses said, 'God advise me.'
God said, 'I advise you of your mother.'
Moses said, 'God advise me.'
God said, 'I advise you of your father.'
*Imam Al-Baqir said, 'For that it is said that two-thirds of
honor is for the mother and one-third is for the father.'* [6]

We reemphasize that what we have discussed related to
rights and obligations is just the legislative minimum that
God has ordained. However, what God recommended is
much more than that, as we will see in the holy narrations.
We will discuss the most important obligations legislated
and recommended which include the following.

First, there is the obligation for spousal support. Many people mistakenly think they are doing their wives a favor when
they provide for them, as if they are giving charity. Providing for the wife is an obligation prescribed by God. Our jurists teach us that. We remember the words of the late
Grand Ayatollah Sayyid Al-Khoei where he said,

*Ongoing spousal support is an obligation on the husband for
food, clothes, shelter, bed, blanket, personal hygiene, and
anything else she needs – as long as he is capable financially. If she leaves, abandoning him without any religious justification, then she becomes undeserving of the spousal support.* [7]

---

[6] Ibid.
[7] Al-Khoei, *Minhaj Al-Saliheen*, 2:287

A husband has a duty to gracefully provide for his wife. It is not merely providing her what she needs to survive. He must be that guardian that protects, provides, and ensures that she is taken care of in all aspects.

As we mentioned, one should not limit himself to the minimal obligation incumbent on him. It is narrated in our traditions that offering more for the family is better than charity. Providing more for the family is important and one has to acknowledge that responsibility and work tirelessly to fulfill it. It will render positive results and bring happiness into his home. It is narrated that Imam Al-Sadiq said,

> Man needs to possess three attributes in his home and with his family, even if they are not naturally part of his personality... nice cohabitation, willingness to be generous but wise, and zealous over one's family.[8]

Of course, the spirit of giving must be balanced and reasonable so one does not go too far where he is forced to drown in debt. A caring wife must pay attention to this issue. She ought not to overburden her husband's shoulders with the justification that she is entitled to spousal support. Spousal support must be within the reasonable and legitimate religious guidelines. It should not become wasteful, which is abhorred, and can contribute to ruining the relationship.

Secondly, a wife has a right to intimate relations with her husband. The husband is obligated to make himself available to his wife at least once every four months, or whatever shorter period that would protect her from falling into sin. At first glance, one might say that this is unfair to women.

---

[8] Al-Majlisi, *Bihar Al-Anwar*, 75:236

However, this is again a bare minimum and as we mentioned previously we should work to observe more than the bare minimum placed before us. There are numerous narrations and traditions that speak of the great reward in being available for your spouse, equating it to the reward of one who struggles in the way of God. Husbands must be mindful that what they do for their wives, especially in regards to intimacy, contributes greatly to the contentment in their relationship and the overall health of the marriage.

Thirdly, women have a right to be treated with dignity and respect by their husbands. It is an There is no excuse otherwise. He must refrain from insulting or humiliating her, and must not engage in any kind of abuse – be it physical, emotional, or psychological. There are narrations that explicitly prohibit harming and hurting women. The Prophet said, "God and his messenger are innocent from he who harms a woman until she abandons him."[9] Imam Al-Sadiq is also narrated to have said, "May God have mercy on a servant that does good between him and his wife..."[10]

Fourthly, a wife is entitled to friendship and companionship with her husband. Good companionship is different than respect. A man must build a relationship with his wife that is based on respect and compassion. He must treat her as a dignified person with feelings and emotions. At the same time, he must look at her as a friend and companion. Here we must emphasize several key points.

Kind words: A man must speak to his wife with kind words that reflect a sense of compassion and affection. The

---

[9] Ibid, 73:366.
[10] Al-Amili, *Wasa'el al-Shia*, 14:122.

Prophet is narrated to have said, "The statement - I love you - by a man to a woman [i.e. his wife] will never be removed from her heart."[11] Unfortunately, some men don't even take the time to express these simple words. With these effortless words, a person can earn the love and compassion of the closest person to him. A kind word goes a long way, let alone with the person that is closest to you. As the Prophet instructed, "O Abathar, a kind word is charity."[12]

Not being neglectful: It is imperative that a man gives his wife proper attention and does not make her feel neglected. He must be proactive in reassuring her that she is a priority and an integral part of his life.

Looking attractive for her: It is a right of the women for her husband to look attractive for her. Similar to how the man desires for his wife to look in the best possible way for him, he needs to reciprocate that to her. We find that there is a narration transmitted by Al-Hassan Ibn Jaham where he says;

> *I once saw Imam Ali Al-Rida and noticed that he had dyed his hair. I said, 'May I be sacrificed for you, why have you dyed your hair?' He replied, 'Yes. Indeed, preparation [of a man to look attractive for his wife] increases modesty in women. Women abandoned modesty when their spouses abandoned preparation.' Then he said, 'Will you be content if you see her in the same state she sees you when you are not prepared?' I said 'No.' He said, 'It is the same [for her].*[13]

---

[11] Ibid, 14:10.

[12] Ibid, 3:507.

[13] Ibid, 14:183.

Imam Al-Sadiq is also narrated to have said,

> *Three things are indispensable for a man in his relationship with his wife. They are: agreement with a woman so he can obtain her satisfaction, love, and affection; good manners in dealing with her; and engendering her affection by looking attractive in her eyes and providing more for her.*[14]

Creating a good environment: We find that some men - due to the struggles of work and hardships of life - release all of their negativity and frustration inside the house. Instead of bringing joy to the family when he arrives to the home, he becomes a reason for their misery.

He might demand calmness and request no one talk to him because he desires to rest. Although he has a right to rest and relax at home, it should not be at the cost of the closest people to him. A man is obligated as the head of the household to tend to the needs of his family members and to make sure they are doing well. Unfortunately, we find that some men spend more time outside the home where they display good manners and carry a positive attitude, yet, as soon as they come home, they expect everyone to go to sleep and to be unbothered by any requests. This is wrong as is illustrated by the Prophet where he says, "A man sitting with his family is more desirable to God Almighty than retreating in this mosque of mine [to worship]."[15]

Serving the wife and children: It is noticeable that many men disdain working at home and helping their wives. A man might mistakenly think that his wife was created only

---

[14] Al-Majlisi, *Bihar Al-Anwar*, 75:237.

[15] Al-Reyshahri, *Mizan Al-Hikma*, 2:1186.

to serve him and his only job is to issue orders. This is contrary to the examples set by the Prophet and Imam Ali. The Commander of the Faithful always helped Lady Zahra with household chores and that did not diminish from his status. In fact, the noble narrations make it clear that serving the wife and children is only done by the best of the best. The Prophet states, "No one serves the family except the believer, martyr, and a man who God desires for him the good in this life and hereafter."[16]

Thus, a man who serves his family and aids them at home has special attributes. He is either a believer, martyr, or one that God desires for him the good in this life and hereafter. Truly, this is a lofty and honorable status. As to the misconception that a man working at home belittles his status, this notion is the result of baseless traditions and ignorant customs that have been passed down generationally. These traditions still have an impact on people although they contradict the moral and religious teachings.

Fifth, a man must be patient and forgiving with his wife. Two people living together, with different habits and perspectives, are bound to have some tension and disagreement. It is only natural. Keeping this in mind, forgiveness and patience need to be utilized in the relationship. A man is his wife's guardian and protector. To truly serve in that role, the husband is obligated to employ patience and manage the disagreement or conflict that takes place in his household. It is his responsibility and her right that he takes patience as his policy.

---

[16] Al-Majlisi, *Bihar Al-Anwar*, 101:132.

Consequently, a wife is entitled to this right from her husband. God calls for treating women with mercy as the Prophet includes women as a class of individuals that we have to be particularly conscious and respectful of. He said, "Fear God with the two weak [groups in society]; the orphans and women. Surely, the best amongst you is the best in treatment to his family."[17] Manhood is not displayed by the strength of one's fist nor of the loudness of one's voice. It is shown through one's compassion and patience, especially with the people closest to you.

THE RIGHTS OF A HUSBAND

In addition to His emphasis on the wife's rights and what she is entitled to, God also granted the husband rights that must be honored and fulfilled by his wife. He established a set of etiquettes and instructions that a wife should adhere to in her relationship with her husband.

For one, conceding to the husband in his guardianship over the household is vital for his success in managing the home. This is notwithstanding the fact that we find examples of men who fail in fulfilling their obligations. Furthermore, many women surpass their husbands in their ability to take charge of certain roles and duties. Nonetheless, divine legislation looks at the general conditions that transcend time and not the exceptions or what might apply in specific circumstances.

The two primary rights that are obligatory for a wife to observe with her husband pertaining to sexual intimacy and

---

[17] Al-Majlisi, *Bihar Al-Anwar*, 76:268

consent. Others rights discussed may not be obligatory but are strongly recommended and have a considerable impact on the husband and wife.

Right to Intimacy

Sexual intimacy is a big part of marriage, something that is sacred to the institution of marriage and cannot be practiced outside of that relationship. One of the rights of the husband is that his wife be intimately available for him when he needs her, except in times when it is impermissible for her to have sex (i.e. primarily during her menstrual period). Abu Baseer narrates that Imam Al-Sadiq said, "A woman came to the Messenger of God and asked what the right of a husband on his wife is? The Prophet replied, to fulfill his [sexual] needs..."[18] This is the primary right of the husband.

A healthy sex life between husband and wife is key to a successful marriage. It is important to keep in mind that a relationship does not stop at observing rights and obligations, nor is it cut dry to receive and not reciprocate. Though a wife has this obligation to her husband, the husband also has the obligation to treat her with respect, honor, and consideration. Successful healthy marriages are not born out of merely demanding for one's rights, it comes through communication and being sensitive of each other's wants and needs. It is a two-way street. But to know how to navigate that street, you have to know what is expected of you and the person you're meeting along that road.

Furthermore, when it comes to this particular right it is important for women to be aware of a couple things. For one,

---

[18] Al-Amili, *Wasa'el al-Shia*, 14:122.

the wife must make a genuine effort to be pleasant, present-able, or personable within the context of sexual intimacy with her husband, as with the husband towards his wife. If certain things, especially relating to hygiene for example, may turn her husband off they should be avoided. The same applies to the husbands. Do not allow yourself to carry re-pellants for your spouse. The smallest things can have an impact in this regard. Secondly, abstaining from recom-mended fasting may need to be practiced if it compromises their sexual relationship. It is better for a wife to fulfill the needs of her husband than fast. Therefore, if the wife knows that fasting a recommended fast would compromise this part of the relationship and her obligation toward her husband then she should not fast at that time. Muhammad Ibn Muslim narrates the words of Imam Al-Baqir who de-scribed a conversation between a woman and the Holy Prophet.

> *A woman came to the Messenger of God and asked, 'O Messenger of God, what is the right of a husband on his wife?' He replied, '... She should not voluntarily fast with-out his permission and to not make herself unavailable to him...* [19]

Consent of the Husband

Husbands are expected to be guardians and protectors of their homes. They are the sentinels of their families, their wives, and their children. The wife plays a huge role in being the primary supporter and partner in her husband's life, es-pecially when it comes to their home. In light of that, com-

---

[19] Al-Amili, *Wasa'el Al-Shia*, 14:112

munication and consent is an integral part of having a successful relationship. The wife is expected not to go places that her husband does not want her to go or to leave at times that he does not desire for her to leave. In essence, there must be communication and consent from her husband. Imam Ja'far Al-Sadiq is narrated to have said,

> *The Messenger of God prohibited a woman from leaving the house without her husband's consent. If she leaves [without his consent], every angel in the skies and every creation from the jinn and mankind will curse her until she returns home. The Prophet prohibited her from beautifying herself before others except her husband. If she does [beautify herself before others], it is God's right to burn her in hellfire.[20]*

The wisdom behind this rule could be two-fold. First, to ensure that the woman's outings do not compromise the man's right to sexual intimacy with his wife. Second, this right is meant for the husband to use to protect his wife from inadvertently putting herself in a situation that can compromise her modesty or honor. Men are aware of other men in a way that women may not be. A man's role is to protect his wife from being hurt or harmed by others.

The purpose of this right is both educational and ethical. It gives the husband and wife an opportunity to learn about each other, their expectations, and what they like and dislike. In particular, when the husband does not give his wife consent to go somewhere specific it is a good chance to explain why that is so that the wife is aware of it and will avoid it altogether in the future. The husband needs to remind

---

[20] Al-Sadouq, *Man La Yahdaruh Al-Faqih*, 4:6.

himself of this purpose when exercising this right. If the man exercises this right and deprives his wife from leaving the house for no legitimate reason, then he would be arbitrarily abusing this right and acting unjustly. Successful marriages cannot come to fruition like that, they have to be based on mutual consideration, respect, and empathy. Any form of abuse or imbalance in exercising one's rights on both sides will compromise the relationship.

It is unfortunate to see that in some households the home has become nothing more than a place to sleep at night. It is not a home, merely a hotel of sorts. The spouses spend all their time and energy doing things for other people but each other. The wife is out all day and neglects her husband while tending to the needs or whims of friends and family. The husband is responsible to prevent these situations from developing. He can use his right of disallowing his wife from certain outings to manage the affairs of his home. When there is communication and consent, the wife is likely to be wiser in her decision-making and avoid going places that do not keep her home a priority. Of course, this right is granted to the man so he preserve his household, not destroy it.

Service and Patience

Another important matter that God particularly emphasizes repeatedly is a woman's work inside the home, serving her husband and children. Although working inside the home is not a religious obligation for a woman, it is revered by God and she is greatly rewarded for the smallest acts inside her home.

Historically, in most nations and communities, the woman played the lead role inside the home. She assumed the duties of cooking, cleaning, and caring for the children. Most communities find that this sort of housework was the natural obligation of the woman. However, Islam removes this obligation from the woman and grants her the full right to decide not to perform any work inside the home. But, when a woman chooses to take care of the home, which she almost always does and does so brilliantly, God rewards her in bounties. It is one thing to fulfill our obligations and God honors us for that. It is another thing to go above and beyond our duties and our wives and mothers do that every single day. She gets rewarded for it because it is volunteer work. Islam relied on two main characteristics in the woman that makes her willing and capable of assuming the noble role of taking care of the home.

First, she has the undying spirit of love, compassion, and giving that is rooted in her heart of hearts. Second, there is a true promise from God rewarding her for her unequivocal service. The noble narrations encourage the wife to offer her service to her husband and promises her for that great reward and recompense. One of the countless narrations that alludes to this is by Imam Al-Sadiq. He said,

> *A righteous woman is better than one thousand non-righteous men... any woman that serves her husband for seven days, God will close seven gates of hellfire for her, and will open eight gates of heaven for her to decide which one to enter through.*[21]

On another occasion Imam Al-Sadiq brought a specific example of how great it is for a woman to do even the sim-

---

[21] Al-Amili, *Wasa'el Al-Shia*, 14:123.

plest of things for her husband, like giving him a drink of water.

> *If a woman quenches her husband's thirst with a drink of water, that is better for her than a year's worth of worship, fasting the day and standing in worship through the night, and God will build for her every time she quenches her husband's thirst, a city in paradise, and will forgive sixty sins of hers.*[22]

In a third narration Imam Al-Sadiq relayed that Um Salama asked the Holy Prophet what the reward would be for women who serve their husbands. The Holy Prophet said,

> *Any woman that removes an object in her husband's home from one place to another, desiring goodness in it, God will surely look at her [with mercy], and whoever God looks at [with mercy], He will not punish.*[23]

Service brings great reward and so does patience. There is no doubt that the differences that exist between a couple's habits and manners impacts their marriage. If the husband and wife do not develop some type of patience in overcoming some of the challenges they encounter, the marriage will inevitably fail. The teachings of Ahlulbayt not only instruct the man to be patient and forgiving with his wife, but also call for the wife to exercise patience with her husband and endure the hardships that come with marriage. The narrations specifically focus on two forms of patience.

One, a woman that exercises patience when she is being mistreated by her husband. Even if the husband is oppress-

---

[22] Ibid.
[23] Al-Tousi, *Al-Amaali*, 618

ing and violating the wife's rights, when the wife shows patience, God will reward her immensely in the hereafter. Her patience will preserve the family – the pillar for the community – and may even guide the husband to mend his ways. Displaying patience in these types of situations is a form of struggle in the way of God, "The [most important] struggle for a woman comes in good companionship [to her husband]." Imam Al-Sadiq alludes to this in a beautiful narration.

> *The punishment of the grave will be alleviated from three types of women, and their place in the hereafter will be with Lady Fatima the Daughter of Muhammad: a woman patient with her husband's protectiveness, a woman patient with her husband's ill manners, and a woman who gifts her dowry to her husband. God will grant each one rewards equivalent to one thousand martyrs, and will write for each one the worship of one year.*[24]

Two, exercising patience in serving her husband and family in addition to enduring any hardships that are the result of the husband's financial struggles. This form of patience is also encompassed by the tradition on good companionship above. God will reward the wife substantially for being patient and perseverant during trying times for the husband. The Holy Prophet speaks about this in a conversation with a woman named Al-Hawla. She approached him and asked him about the rights of the husband. He replied,

> *Hawla, it is incumbent on the woman to be patient with her husband [in times of] harm and benefit, and to exercise pa-*

---

[24] Al-Amili, *Wasa'el Al-Shia*, 15:37.

*tience [in times of] hardship and ease, like the wife of the
tried Jacob.*

*She was patient, serving him for 18 years carrying him on
her shoulders like all the other carriers, grinding with the
grinders, washing with the washers, and offering him food
that he ate and praised God the Almighty. She used to
wrap him in a blanket and carry him on her shoulders, out
of sympathy and kindness for the sake of God, and seeking
closeness to Him the Almighty.*

*O Hawla, by the One who sent me with the truth as a
prophet and messenger, every woman that is patient with her
husband during times of hardship and ease, and is obedient
to him and his commands, God will place her in the hereafter with the wife of Job.*[25]

The discussion on the rights of husband and wife is im-
mense and would need even greater detail than provided
here. This aims to serve an overview to provide benefit to
husbands and wives in observing their obligations towards
one another. It is a reminder to be conscious of one another
and realize that these rights and obligations are not meant to
dictate a relationship, they're merely safety valves – bare
minimums to make sure you are taken care of. Otherwise,
love and compassion rule. And that only mandates the best
of treatment of one another.

---

[25] Al-Nouri, *Mustadrak Al-Wasa'el*, 14:242.

CHALLENGES IN MARRIAGE

In the name of God, the most Beneficent, the most Merciful

Surely the men who submit and the women who submit, and the believing men and the believing women, and the obeying men and the obeying women, and the truthful men and the truthful women, and the patient men and the patient women and the humble men and the humble women, and the almsgiving men and the almsgiving women, and the fasting men and the fasting women, and the men who guard their private parts and the women who guard, and the men who remember God much and the women who remember-- God has prepared for them forgiveness and a mighty reward.[1]

After discussing the religious rights that each spouse has in a marriage, we need to discuss two important matters. First, the issue of equality between men and women. There is the notion that men have more rights than women and are superior. Second, the matter when a spouse violates the rights of the other, which the Holy Quran describes as a form of

---

[1] The Holy Quran. Chapter 33. [The Clans; Arabic: *Al-Ahzab*]. Verse 35.

disobedience. In this chapter we should answer the following questions.

- What are the religious consequences in these situations of disobedience?
- How should a person deal with their spouse if he or she violates their rights?
- Which rights specifically, if violated, constitute disobedience?
- Is any violation of rights or lack in fulfilling obligations considered disobedience?

By answering these questions, we will gain some insight on what God legislates to be a violation of rights and what is considered to be disobedience.

EQUALITY BETWEEN MEN AND WOMEN

When we examine religious rulings, it seems as if there is inequality with regards to the rights that men and women have to observe. The enemies of Islam attempt to misuse various examples to perpetuate this narrative - the cornerstone of which is that Islam does not afford women rights. They bolster this argument with the following verse from the Holy Quran, "Men are the protectors and maintainers of women, because God has given the one more [strength] than the other..."[2]

They claim this verse shows a clear preference for men over women. There are other examples that support this concept of preference, they argue. For example, men are permitted

---

[2] The Holy Quran. Chapter 4. [The Women; Arabic: *Al-Nisaa*]. Verse 34.

to marry multiple wives, women are prohibited from assuming certain jobs, and that only the husband has the authority to divorce. In this chapter, we are not aiming to rebut these baseless arguments that these individuals bring forth. What we attempt to discuss is whether Islam truly favors men over women by granting him more rights and power. To answer this question, we need to address a series of issues, all of which will demonstrate that this narrative is baseless, misleading, and wrong.

Cannon Law Not Civil Law

The laws that prescribed the rights, obligations, and powers to men and women are divine law that are not subject to whims of man. God does not have kinship with anyone, nor does He have a gender. A person can only seek nearness to Him through piety and worship. It is senseless to say that God favors men over women or likes one gender more. God does not oppress anyone, because He is Just. This is the foundation of our creed. It is necessary on a theological level to understand the flow of God's law to us. Man-made customs and traditions can be debunked, but once we have established that something is truly from God – via revelation or His prophets – we accept it and submit to it. If something does not conform to our own likings or whims then the issue is with us, not God's law. It may be difficult to swallow, but this is a consistent issue in this area of study and many others within faith and society.

Conflict in Interests

There is no doubt that conflict in interests is unavoidable. Interests conflict and clash with one another. God always gives priority to that which renders a greater benefit than that which produces less benefit. He prevents that which yields great harm, even though some people might be unaffected by the harm and moreover, gain a net benefit. This is illustrated in the Holy Quran, "They ask you about intoxicants and games of chance. Say, in both of them there is a great sin and means of profit for men, and their harm is greater than their profit."[3]

Since the harm is more dominant, the minimal benefits are not significant enough to sanction it. Thus, the act becomes impermissible because there is a greater interest in the impermissibility than the permissibility. Building on this concept, we can attain a better understanding of many of the religious rulings which might appear to pass on a particular benefit.

God the Almighty with His knowledge and wisdom always views an act as a whole and looks for what has a greater benefit and serves a better interest for people. This applies to many of the rulings related to marriage where there is a conflict in interest.

The Religious Law: Between Compulsion and Understanding

The religious rulings provide a framework to organize social relationships. This framework includes rights and obligations. Islam calls for people to use dialogue and understanding to enjoy their rights from one another as opposed to force or compulsion. Our faith desires to foster mercy and love between people that are exchanging rights and obligations. We find that God outlines the specific right or obliga-

---

[3] The Holy Quran. Chapter 2. [The Cow; Arabic: *Al-Baqarah*]. Verse 219.

tion but then instructs the different parties involved to use positive means of communication to reach a mutual understanding on the matter. A remarkable example of this is mentioned explicitly in the Holy Quran where God addresses the retribution for murder and then encourages pardoning,

> *O you who believe, retaliation is prescribed for you in the cases of murder, the free for the free, and the slave for the slave, and the female for the female, but if any remission is made to any one by his (aggrieved) brother, then prosecution (for the bloodwit) should be made according to usage, and payment should be made to him in a good manner... this is an alleviation from your Lord and a mercy, so whoever exceeds the limit after this he shall have a painful chastisement.*[4]

This advocacy for general forgiveness and pardoning is also exhibited in another verse where God says,

> *And the recompense of evil is punishment like it, but whoever forgives and amends, he shall have his reward from God... surely He does not love the unjust. And whoever defends himself after being oppressed, against such there is no cause of blame.*[5]

Guardianship: An Obligation and Responsibility

Islam's theory on administration and responsibility is drastically different than materialistic civilizations. In materialistic civilizations, it is admirable for people to compete and strive

---

[4] The Holy Quran. Chapter 2. [The Cow; Arabic: *Al-Baqarah*]. Verse 178.

[5] The Holy Quran. Chapter 42. [The Consultation; Arabic: *Al-Shura*]. Verse 40-41.

for leadership positions. On the other hand, Islam views guardianship and administration as a religious obligation that is not attained through competition.

It becomes religiously obligatory on anyone who finds himself qualified and capable to assume the position. Islam discourages people to be consumed in competing for things that may have a negative worldly effect on us. We should always strive to strike a balance and live in moderation to attain success in both worlds.

This theory applies to the issue of guardianship in a family. Since the man possesses specific qualities and characteristics that are suitable for leading and managing the family, God put the burden on him to assume this responsibility. The man becomes responsible and accountable before God to do everything in his capacity to take care of his family members. Thus, the holy verse "...because God has given the one more [strength] than the other..."[6], is not speaking about a form of favoritism or preference given to men such that men are better. Rather, God is referring to man's responsibility in his position as a guardian. The only scale that God employs to assess people's rank is their piety as he explains in the Holy Quran, "Verily the most honored of you in the sight of God is the most righteous of you."[7]

It is important to realize that leader in any facet in this life is not necessarily superior to his subjects. Someone that is inferior in position or status can have a higher standing with God. Consequently, a man who assumes the positon of

---

[6] The Holy Quran. Chapter 4. [The Women; Arabic: *Al-Nisaa*]. Verse 34.

[7] The Holy Quran. Chapter 49. [The Inner Apartments; Arabic: *Al-Hujraat*]. Verse 13.

leading the family and taking care of their affairs is not necessarily the most righteous in God's eyes.

Recompense for Deprivation

If the Lord deprived the woman from assuming certain positions, and offered them to a man, a question can be asked: does a man have a better pathway to seeking closeness to God than a woman because he has greater obligations and more opportunities to do good? One of the women of the Ansar posed this very question to the Prophet. Asmaa bint Yazeed Al-Ansaria came forward to the Prophet while he was amongst his companions. She said,

> *May my father and mother be sacrificed for you. I have come to you as a delegate from the believing women. I know that there is no woman, in the East or West, that would have listened to what I have said and will not share my opinion. God has sent you as the truth for men and women, so we have believed in you and in your Lord that sent you. We women are confined and limited to our homes, satisfying men's pleasures, and carrying their children. Men have been favored by God over us with Fridays [i.e. by performing Friday prayers] and social gatherings, visiting the sick, and participating in funerals... If they go out on a mission, we protect their money, sow their clothes, and raise their children. Do we not have a share in the good deeds with you O' Messenger of God?*

After listening intently to the woman's plea, the Holy Prophet turned towards his companions and asked, "Have you heard better words from a woman inquiring about her faith than this?" All pleasantly surprised, they replied that they had not. The Prophet turned back to the woman and said,

> *Go, O' Asmaa, and inform the women with you that a woman who is a good spouse to her husband, seeks his contentment, and adheres to his acceptance, is equal to all of the acts of men that you have mentioned.*

The woman left cheering and shouting "God is Great" in celebration.[8]

Many of the accusations against Islam and its mistreatment of women are baseless. In fact, Islam regards women and embraces their rights more than any other civilization. Indeed, Islam did create restrictions around Muslim woman, not to confine her role in the world, but rather to repel corruption and shield her from anything that can compromise her honor and purity.

The mischaracterization of Islam and women can be traced back to the some of the improper practices championed by some Muslims. These practices are incorrectly perceived as based in religion when they are in fact culturally inspired. However, Islam is firm in combating any backwards practices and dispelling notions about guardianship and the rights of women.

This is in addition to the relentless attacks by Islam's adversaries who make an effort at every turn to undermine Islamic theology and portray it as at odds with the advancement and prosperity of women. Unfortunately, some Muslims

---

[8] Al-Siyouti, *Al-Dur Al-Manthur*, 2:153.

have bought into this distorted narrative because they blindly believe what is popular in mainstream culture.

Today, mainstream culture has portrayed women as one of two extremes. Either she unreservedly projects her beauty and sexuality and is objectified by her environment, or she assumes the role of a man and does away with her femininity. Both extremes are rejected because they both sacrifice essential elements of a woman's character and virtue. Islam promotes women's education, career development, and general advancement. It is not against women seeking high positions and roles in politics, media, business, academia, or any other field. However, the key is that they pursue these roles without sacrificing their modesty and virtue. This, in essence, is applicable to all people – men and women alike.

DISOBEDIENCE: CAUSES AND REMEDIES

The violation of rights or failure in fulfilling obligations by either spouse is considered to be disobedience. God has legislated for every disobedience by the husband or wife a specific judgement. For example, if the husband does not fulfill his obligation towards his family by failing to provide for them, the wife has two options. Either she negotiates an agreement with her husband where she concedes or waives her right or she files a grievance with the religious jurist. The jurist will assess the case and if he concludes that the husband has failed in fulfilling his obligations, he will compel the husband to either provide the financial dues or divorce. There are other rulings that apply in different cases of disobedience that are beyond the scope of this discussion.

Nonetheless, in all cases of conflict or disagreement between the husband and wife, it is critical to keep the following pointers in mind. First, family conflicts should remain between the two spouses and should not leave the household. The husband and wife should consult the religious rulings and teachings to resolve their disputes.

Second, the husband and wife should adopt the proper religious means to resolve their disputes. One of those important tools is when a conflict reaches a breaking point, each spouse should select an arbitrator. These arbitrators can mediate between the two spouses and help them reach a mutual understanding. This instruction is provided for in the Holy Quran.

> *And if you fear a breach between the two, then appoint a judge from his people and a judge from her people; if they both desire agreement, God will bring harmony between them, surely God is Knowing, Aware.*[9]

Third, it is essential that neither spouse abuse their rights by exercising them abusively. The couple cannot become heedless and forget that the Almighty is overseeing and monitoring everything we do. God reminds us that nothing escapes Him in the Holy Quran, "Do not seek a way against them; surely God is High, Great."[10]

In another moving verse, He states, "And if you do good (to others) and guard (against evil), then surely God is aware of what you do."[11] Conflicts and disputes are inevitable in

---

[9] The Holy Quran. Chapter 4. [The Women; Arabic: *Al-Nisaa*]. Verse 35.

[10] The Holy Quran. Chapter 4. [The Women ; Arabic: *Al-Nisaa*]. Verse 34.

[11] The Holy Quran. Chapter 4. [The Women ; Arabic: *Al-Nisaa*]. Verse 128.

family. However, there is a divine prescription on how to resolve them. We must commit to this prescription and adopt the means and ways that God has provided for us to address our marital problems.

EXCESSIVE OBEDIENCE

The other side of the token is excessive obedience to your spouse whereby it is done at the cost of disobeying God. Although this is applicable with both the husband or wife, it is especially manifested when the wife excessively obeys her husband. The Holy Quran describes this situation, "Whoever exceeds the limits of God, such are wrong-doers."[12]

Unfortunately, many men coerce their wives to ignore or go against what is prescribed in the religion. A common example of this comes with the hijab. Some men forbid their wives from wearing the hijab or encourage them to dress less modestly. This often trickles down to their daughters, which itself has its own ramifications. The wife concedes to her husband's wishes thinking that it is justified because she is obeying him. We need to be aware that obedience to one's spouse has a limit and such a justification does not hold water. When obedience of another is in disobedience of God it is not acceptable.

All in all, disobedience and excessive obedience are both wrong. When the husband or wife engages in such acts, they are dishonoring themselves and distancing themselves from God. A righteous husband and wife need to be aware of their religious rights and duties and exercise them in con-

---

[12] The Holy Quran. Chapter 4. [The Cow ; Arabic: *Al-Baqarah*]. Verse 229.

formity with what God legislated. This is necessary for the health of their relationship and even more so in creating the environment that they will raise their children in.

RAISING A CHILD

In the name of God, the most Beneficent, the most Merciful

*And certainly We created man of an extract of clay, then
We made him a small seed in a firm resting-place, then We
made the seed a clot, then We made the clot a lump of flesh,
then We made (in) the lump of flesh bones, then We clothed
the bones with flesh, then We caused it to grow into another
creation, so blessed be God, the best of the creators. Then after that you will most surely die. Then surely on the day of
resurrection you shall be raised.*[1]

Man is the most honored creation that God created. Hu-
mans are the center of all creation and God's vicegerents on
earth. God gave special care and attention to man by guiding him through all the phases of his life – from the first
moment he opens his eyes to the last breath he takes. Divine care actually commences in the initial stages of creation, before even being born into this world. A fetus is prepared to enter the world where he or she can be raised, nurtured, and developed into a human being. God describes
the formation of a human being in the Holy Quran, "Cer-

---

[1] The Holy Quran. Chapter 23. [The Believers; Arabic: *Al-Muminoon*]. Verse 12.

tainly, We created man in the best make."[2] Physically, spiritually, and intellectually God created us in the best way. It is up to us to capture our God-given potential or throw it away and become the lowest of the low. "Then We relegated him to the lowest of the low,"[3] God says in the next verse.

In this chapter, we will discuss childrearing and shed light on the rights that children have upon their parents. Parents cannot just bring children to this world without rendering proper care – physical, emotional, spiritual, psychological and cognitive. Parents have an obligation to raise, nurture, and guide their children so they can become equipped with the knowledge and morals to lead a successful righteous life. This is the God-given right of our children. The obligations parents must adhere to in order to produce a righteous generation can be classified in three stages: before conception, pregnancy, and after birth.

BEFORE CONCEPTION

The teachings of Islam emphasize both heredity and environment, nature and nurture, in the formation of a child and the molding of his character and manners. The decisions and habits of a parent can have an effect on the child before the child is even conceived. For example, there are traditions pertaining to the quality of food that a parent consumes. Halal and non-halal food do in fact have a substantial impact on the moral state of a person. Thus, Islam emphasizes the importance of being selective with the quality

---

[2] The Holy Quran. Chapter 95. [The Fig; Arabic: *Al-Tin*]. Verse 4.

[3] Ibid, verse 5.

of food we consume because the food will have an effect on a child in his creation physically and spiritually.

There are a host of obligations and manners related to the time of intimacy between the husband and wife, and the effect of this on the creation of a child physically and spiritually. A number of narrations have indicated that the time of sexual intimacy is significant. There are times that are abhorred because of the detrimental effect they have on the creation of a fetus. Moreover, there are sexual acts that are detested for the same reason. It is imperative for a newly married couple to look up these narrations and gain insight on the etiquettes of sexual intimacy, recommended practices such as supplications, desired and abhorred times and acts – because many of these narrations specify the effects of all these factors on the offspring. This is especially relevant when the couple is contemplating having a child.

Some of these factors implicate the physical condition of the child while others affect the mental, psychological, and spiritual dimensions. It is unwise to disparage these narrations and claim they are not scientifically proven. As long as these narrations have a proper chain of narrators and can be traced back to the Ahlulbayt, that is sufficient for us to follow and be mindful of them. At the very minimum, a person should follow them to avoid any potential harm, especially when it is related to something so significant such as one's children and their health. It is advisable to refer back to the Prophet's instructions to Imam Ali about sexual intimacy between the husband and wife and its implications on the offspring.[4] You will find that there are specific times and

---

[4] See: Al-Tabrasi, *Makarim Al-Akhlaq*, Chapter Four (Wedding Manners).

acts that have a connection to things like insanity, deafness, blindness, wickedness, depression, and poverty. It does not hurt to be aware of these traditions and keep them in mind.

PREGNANCY

It is essential to understand the significance of the mother that carries the fetus. As much as the hereditary factors of the father affect the fetus, so do the genes of the mother. Consequently, Islam urges a man to select a righteous wife, factoring in the environment she comes from. Some narrations discourage men to marry from specific tribes because at the time the narrations were narrated, these tribes were immersed in the traditions, customs, and practices of the Age of Ignorance. Other narrations instruct men to not be consumed only with the looks and beauty of a woman.

Islam is concerned with the fetus when it is in its mother's womb because he will be influenced by the environment surrounding him. The physical, mental, and psychological state of the mother will have an impact on the child. If a mother is stable, comfortable, and content, this will reflect positively on the fetus. If she is not, the child will be affected just the same.

It is recommended that the mother remains in a state of purity and recites the Holy Quran because it will instill tranquility in her heart, which will certainly reflect positively on the fetus. It is as God says, "Verily in the remembrance of God do hearts find rest."[5]

---

[5] The Holy Quran. Chapter 13. [The Thunder; Arabic: *Al-Ra'ad*]. Verse 28.

It is proven that the fetus is influenced by external sounds and what better sounds for him to hear than the beautiful words of the Holy Quran and the soothing remembrance of God. Finally, there are narrations that encourage the mother to eat specific foods that also have a positive effect on the physical and mental wellbeing of the child.

For example, the Prophet is narrated to have said, "Feed your pregnant women frankincense[6] for it strengthens the intellect of the child."[7] Of course, there are other foods that are also recommended but this example just goes to show that the Prophet was quite specific and explained how ingesting certain foods would have a direct impact on the child. Therefore, a pregnant mother should be conscious and aware of everything she does and the environment she is in because all of that can impact her child.

GIVING BIRTH

The responsibility on the parents to raise their child commences with birth. The parents' role is to preserve, nurture, and advance their child physically, intellectually, and spiritually. It is a grave responsibility because what is at stake is the wellbeing and success of another human being. There are some key practices to keep in mind when graced with a newborn.

---

[6] Frankincense, also called olibanum, is an aromatic resin used in incense and perfumes, obtained from trees

[7] Al-Tabrasi, *Makarim Al-Akhlaq*, 194.

The Recommended Traditions

The first sound a newborn should hear is the words of Ad-han and Iqama – the longer and shorter calls to prayer, respectively. It is a blessed tradition to recite the Adhan in the newborn's right ear and Iqama in his left ear. What better words for the child to open his ears to than "There is no god but God and Muhammad is His Messenger." Additionally, there are a series of traditions that are recommended such as Al-Aqeeqa[8], circumcision of the baby, and drinking water from Euphrates River. All of these traditions are certain and emphasized in our narrations, especially Al-Aqeeqa. In fact, some narrations say that a newborn's wellbeing is conditioned on it.

Other narrations suggest that a person is conditioned on Al-Aqeeqa on Judgement Day as Imam Al-Sadiq describes, "Every person on the Day of Judgment is contingent on his Aqeeqa, and Al-Aqeeqa is more compulsory than Al-Adhhiya[9]."[10]

The Imams instruct for an Aqeeqa to be fulfilled for a person at any age if it was not done for him when he was a newborn. Omar Ibn Yazeed narrates that he informed Imam Al-Sadiq that he is not aware if his father did an

---

[8] Al-Aqeeqa is a recommended practice in honor of the newborn where the parents slaughter one of three animals – sheep, cow, or camel. It is recommended that this practice is done on the seventh day after the birth of the child and the slaughtered meat is either cooked or distributed, but it is abhorred for the parents or any of their dependents to eat from it. – Eds.

[9] Al-Adhhiya is a recommended practice during Eid Al-Adha where people slaughter one of three animals – sheep, cow, or camel – and distribute to the needy.

[10] Al-Tabrasi, *Makarim Al-Akhlaq*, 226.

Aqeeqa for him or not. The Imam ordered him to do one
and Omar did so even though he was an old man.[11]

Naming the Newborn

A child has a right on his father to give him a good name. It
is incumbent on the father to select an appropriate name
because the name contributes to the formation of the identity of a person. A person's name stays with them for the
rest of their life. The name must be pleasant and not one
that will be detested by the child, because that will detriment
him psychologically. That is why we find that God has instructed the believers to select pleasant meaningful names
for their kids. It is refreshing to witness that many of the
followers of Ahlulbayt name their children after the Holy
Household. We have narrations that advise us that the best
of names is Muhammad. The Prophet said, "Whoever has
three boys and does not name one after me has forsaken
me."[12]

Sulayman Al-Ja'fary narrates, "I heard Abu Al-Hassan saying, 'Poverty will not enter a home that has the name Muhammad, Ahmed, Ali, Hassan, Hussain, Ja'far, Talib, Abdullah, or Fatima for females.'"[13] These names create a sense of
pride in the child as he grows up, which will increase his attachment and connection to the Prophet and his household.
There must be meaning attached to a name because it will
surely have an impact on the individual as they grow up,
given that the first expression of one's identity usually

---

[11] Al-Majlisi, *Bihar Al-Anwar*, 101:120.

[12] Ibid.

[13] Ibid.

comes with one's name. "Who are you?" someone will ask. The usual response is, "My name is…"

Nursing

Nursing certainly plays an integral role in the development of a newborn, both physically and psychologically. This has been suggested by recent studies as well as supported in our prophetic traditions. Our narrations have also suggested that nursing has an everlasting impact on a child psychologically and spiritually.

The Prophet said, "There is no milk better for a child than his mother's milk."[14] Imam Ali would also say, "Select for nursing like you select for marriage, for nursing changes habits."[15]

These narrations are highlighting the critical role of nursing in the nurture and development of a person and thus, it is important to be selective in who one allows to nurse his children if it is not the mother of the child.

It is important to mention the devastating mistake that some mothers make in not nursing their children, especially if there is no legitimate impediment, like an illness. Some mothers prefer to use formula to feed their children for one reason or another. Unless they are hurting their own health or cannot breastfeed, they should be aware that they are compromising the spiritual, psychological, and physical health of the newborn. The baby has a right to be nursed, and we should not deprive babies from that right and the benefits that flow from it.

---

[14] Al-Sadouq, 'Oyun Akhbar Al-Rida, 1:38.

[15] Al-Amili, Wasa'el Al-Shia, 15:188.

Upbringing

One of the greatest duties parents have is to nurture and raise their children according to our Islamic teachings. Families often mix between what the religion teaches and what they have inherited from their culture. Certain cultural things may be acceptable but they are definitely not in Islam. The following are some bad practices that parents employ in raising their children that we need to be rid of.

Physical Abuse. It is common in some communities to use physical force with children. This is absolutely wrong and unacceptable. Physical abuse is never an effective means to discipline children. It is important to build the child's personality and character in a way that builds his self-worth and respects his dignity.

Consequently, God forbade the use of physical force with children, except in very limited circumstances that have extremely specific conditions. Islamic jurisprudence provides that if a parent physically disciplines their child and leaves a mere red mark on any part of their body, they are deemed to have violated the child's rights and is therein obligated to pay damages to the child. These regulations are intended to limit the scope of utilizing force for disciplinary purposes and protecting the child from abuse. We need to understand that our children are sacred and valuable. Unleashing our anger and frustrations on them using physical force is religiously, morally, and legally wrong. The Prophet forbade disciplining children during times of anger.[16] It is narrated that a man approached Imam Al-Kadhim and complained

---

[16] Al-Reyshahri, *Mizan Al-Hikma*, 1:75.

to him about his son. The Imam advised him, "Do not strike him. Ignore him for a bit, but not for too long."[17] We need to find effective means to discipline and teach our children. Physical and verbal abuse will instill fear and resentment in them. It will damage their confidence and self-esteem, which can leave an everlasting detrimental effect on them as they grow older.

Preferring Males over Females. One of the negative tendencies in some communities, which creates sensitivities between siblings, is showing favoritism or preference for boys over girls. This practice, popular during the Age of Ignorance, was staunchly resisted and combated by Islam. The following verse describes the context of the time of the Age of Ignorance and how backwards the prevailing thought was on having a daughter.

> *When news is brought to one of them, of [the birth of] a female [child], his face darkens, and he is filled with inward grief. With shame does he hide himself from his people, because of the bad news he has had. Shall he retain it on [sufferance and] contempt, or bury it in the dust? What an evil [choice] they decide on?[18]*

Our narrations explicitly dispel the misconceptions rooted in some dark minds that men are superior to women. In fact, we have dozens of traditions that mention the blessing and honor of having daughters. Al-Hassan Ibn Saeed Al-Lukhmi narrates,

---

[17] Ibid.
[18] The Holy Quran. Chapter 16. [The Bee; Arabic: *Al-Nahl*]. Verse 58-59.

A friend of ours had a newborn daughter. He walked into [Imam Al-Sadiq] who saw him frustrated with his wife. [The Imam] told him, 'If God revealed to you and gave you the option that either He chooses for you or you choose for yourself the gender of your child, [what would you have?]' The friend replied, 'I would have said O' Lord You choose for me.' The Imam responded, 'God has chosen for you...'[19]

Al-Jaroud Ibn Munther said,

[Imam Al-Sadiq] told me, 'I was informed that you had a [newborn] daughter and you were dissatisfied. Why would you be unhappy when she is like a beautiful flower? And when you are provided her sustenance? And when the Messenger of God was the father of girls?[20]

It is enough to say that the best man revered by Muslims is the Prophet, who was never granted any sons and whose progeny came only through his daughter, the best of all women – Lady Fatima Al-Zahraa.

Preferential Treatment. Another detrimental practice with raising children is preferential treatment. This will foster hatred and discord between the siblings. Our faith promotes equal treatment amongst the siblings because it is a right the children are entitled to. Even the expression of love should be equal and nondiscriminatory. Imam Ali spoke of an incident where the Prophet expressed his sentiment on sibling equality. "The Prophet witnessed a man with two children,

---

[19] Al-Reyshahri, *Mizan Al-Hikma*, 1:75.
[20] Ibid.

kissing one and not the other... the Prophet reprimanded
the man saying 'Why didn't you treat them equally?'"²¹

Mas'ada Ibn Sadaqa narrates that Imam Al-Baqir said,

> *By God I have taken some of my children and sat them on
> my lap, and expressed increased love and gratitude towards
> them, even though the right [of Imamate] is for another of
> my children... but I do this to protect him [i.e. Imam Ja'far
> Al-Sadiq] so that they [his siblings] do not do to him what
> Joseph's brothers did to Joseph.*²²

It is imperative for parents to treat their children equally especially with expressions of love and care, to avoid hurting
any of them and to strengthen the brotherhood between
them. Otherwise, the children will develop hostility that will
compromise their bond and relationship. The equal treatment should also extend to what they are given in necessities and gifts, such that the children are granted the same
things. Al-Nu'man Ibn Basheer describes this in a narration,

> *My father gave me a gift. My mother Umra Bint Rawaha
> said, 'I do not accept this until the Prophet witnesses [and
> approves this].' [My father] went to the Prophet and ad-
> dressed him, 'I gave my son from Umra something and she
> ordered me to make you a witness.' The Prophet said, 'Did
> you give all of your children the same as this?' [My father]
> replied, 'No.' [The Prophet] responded, 'Fear God and be
> just to your children, I will not witness [and approve] an in-
> justice.*²³

---

²¹ Ibid.
²² Ibid.
²³ Ibid.

The children have a right upon their parents to receive equal treatment on all levels and parents are obliged to honor this right, which will only help foster better intra-relations within the family.

Rigid Treatment. Rigid and strict treatment by parents, especially the father, is ineffective and counterproductive. God encourages parents to exhibit love and affection towards their children because that will be the cornerstone for their successful relationships – be it with their parents and siblings or future wife and children. A child will be more receptive and attentive to his parents if he feels their love and compassion. The Prophet said,

> *Whoever kisses his child, God will record him a good deed, and whoever makes him happy, God will make him merry on Judgement Day. And whoever teaches his children the Holy Quran, the two parents will be called on Judgement Day and they will wear two garments that will radiate light to lighten the faces of the people of paradise...*[24]

In another narration, a man came to the Prophet and talked to him about his family. During the conversation he told the Prophet, "I have never kissed my child." When the man left, the Prophet stated, "This person for me is from the residents of hellfire."[25] Furthermore, we have narrations that encourage parents to step down to their children's level and play and joke with them. The Prophet alludes to this, "Whoever has a boy should go down to his level."[26] The Prophet who is our perfect guide led by example. The com-

---

[24] Ibid.
[25] Ibid.
[26] Al-Amili, *Wasa'el Al-Shia*, 15:203.

panions would frequently witness the Prophet playing with his two grandsons – an inspiration to them and all of us. If parents are able to foster a strong bond with their children, they will be more successful in raising and teaching them because they will be more open and receptive to them. All of this will contribute to a healthier and more positive development of his character and personality.

Discipline and Teaching. A child has a right to be taught noble manners and values by his parents. The parents ought to impart the knowledge that a child needs to decipher right from wrong and to chart a path towards wholesome living. Thus, teaching a child about God and his faith should be a top priority. Abdullah Ibn Fathala relays the following narration,

> If a child reaches the age of three tell him to say seven times 'There is no god but God'.... When he completes seven years, he should be told, 'Wash your face and hands,' if he washes them, he should be told, 'Pray'... If he learns ablution and prayer [at the age of nine], God will forgive his parents – God Willing.[27]

The discussion on teaching and educating children is extensive. Various narrations call on parents to teach and train their kids to follow *Makarim Al-Alkhlaq* – the best of ethics and virtues. However, during our contemporary times, many parents have unfortunately shifted their focus to teaching their children non-Islamic manners and traditions.

We find that some parents are concerned with teaching their children foreign languages, while neglecting Arabic –

---

[27] Al-Sadouq, *Al-Amaali*, 475.

the language of the Holy Quran, dressing their children with foreign brand names, and exposing them to non-Islamic traditions. This does a great disservice to our children because it distances them from their Islamic roots and heritage. This demonstrates a lack in our identity which will reflect negatively on our kids and their future. Of course, we must integrate within our societies and be a part of the new communities that we live in. However, we must hold on to our identity and heritage. Integration with preservation is our path – not assimilation nor isolation.

Thus, it is so important to hold on to our roots and teach our kids to do the same. We have to assume our responsibility towards our children and take advantage of their young age and pure souls to impart the love and knowledge of the Holy Quran and Prophetic traditions. We need to teach them to espouse the words of the Holy Quran and hold on firm to the traditions of Ahlulbayt.

The Prophet is narrated to have said, "Teach your children three things: the love of your Prophet, the love of Ahlulbayt, and the recitation of the Holy Quran."[28] Imam Al-Sadiq also teaches us to instill in our children the spirit giving and goodness. He says, "Teach the child to give charity whether it be a piece [of bread], a handful [of food], or anything no matter how small."[29]

---

[28] Al-Reyshahri, *Mizan Al-Hikma*, 4:3680.

[29] Al-Amili, *Wasa'el Al-Shia*, 6:261.

.

PARENTS

In the name of God, the most Beneficent, the most Merciful

The Lord has decreed that you worship none but Him, and that you be kind to parents. Whether one or both of them attain old age in their life, say not to them a word of contempt, nor repel them, but address them in terms of honor. And, out of kindness, lower to them the wing of humility, and say: 'My Lord, have mercy on them both as they did care for me when I was little.'[1]

God engineered the human being to live and function as part of a larger community. The connection to others is not merely found physically or socially, but deeply rooted in the spiritual foundation of the human being. It is embedded in God's instructions for spiritual worship. For example, congregational prayers are much more recommended than solitary prayers and render a much greater reward. Islam made the sense of community a priority perhaps because God desires for mankind to move and grow together, rather than separately.

---

[1] The Holy Quran. Chapter 17. [The Night Journey; Arabic: *Al-Israa*]. Verse 23-24.

Thus, a person cannot seek true closeness to God in isolation. He must function within a social framework where he has rights and obligations. That framework includes fellow citizens, neighbors, colleagues, friends, and family members. The first and foremost social circle in that framework is our parents. The structure is one of layers, with varying levels of rights and obligations. The closer the layer the greater the obligations towards those parties. The core layer which includes the parents has more rights and obligations than the second layer, the rest of the family. The family has more rights and obligations than the third layer, the extended relatives, and so on and so forth.

All of these layers in society aim to help a person on his journey towards God. The Prophet says, "All of you are guardians, and all of you are responsible for your subjects."[2] A believer needs to be conscious and aware of his duties and obligations towards every person at every layer in his social framework. Let us take the time to delve into the relationship with the parents, which is the most important relationship of them all.

HOW TO TREAT YOUR PARENTS

If we examine the holy verse we began the chapter with, we find a number of key points to keep in mind. Firstly, God mentions the word 'qada' which can be translated as 'decreed' or 'ordained'. In Arabic, the word 'qada' has a greater level of emphasis and finality than 'amar' which is translated as 'ordered'. 'Amar' is subject to discussion and debate.

---

[2] Al-Majlisi, *Bihar Al-Anwar*, 72:38.

However, 'qada' is a final non-negotiable command. Thus, doing good unto one's parents is a final decree that is not debatable.

Secondly, doing good unto one's parents is one of the most significant decrees that God revealed through His divine messages. Doing good unto parents is tied directly to the worship of God. The Quranic phrase *'you worship none but Him'* included an affirmation and negation to limit worship exclusively to the Almighty. It then continues to mention one of the most important acts of worship – doing good unto our parents.

Thirdly, the terms 'parents' and 'doing good' are used in the absolute sense, implying that 'doing good' is encompassing of any form of goodness and not limited to one particular kind of good act. Anything that constitutes good must be done towards the parents; whether they are Muslims or not, near or far, alive or deceased.

The Holy Quran mentions doing good to one's parents in four chapters. In each chapter, the mentioning came directly after the mention of Tawhid[3], which is another indicator of its great significance. The four verses are as follows;

> *And when We made a covenant with the children of Israel, you shall not serve any but God and [you shall do] good to [your] parents.[4]*
> *And serve God and do not associate anything with Him and be good to the parents.[5]*

---

[3] Tawhid means the oneness of God, and is the first pillar of Islam. – Eds.
[4] The Holy Quran. Chapter 2. [The Cow; Arabic: *Al-Baqarah*]. Verse 83.
[5] The Holy Quran. Chapter 4. [The Woman; Arabic: *Al-Nisaa*]. Verse 36.

*Say come I will recite what your Lord has forbidden to you,
that you do not associate anything with Him and show
kindness to your parents.*[6]
The Lord has decreed that you worship none but Him.[7]

This repeated association between Tawhid and doing good
unto parents further underscores the importance of this
matter in God's eyes. It reinforces the fact that our relationship with our parents is directly linked to our worship, and
thus God's pleasure is connected to the contentment of our
parents with us.

THE RIGHTS OF PARENTS

After establishing the importance of doing good unto parents as an act of worship, we can get into some of the details regarding the rights of our parents. In addition, we will
touch on how to do good towards them and the extent to
which we need to obey them.

How to Deal with our Parents?

The general manner in which we deal with our parents
should be characterized by subservience. Islam uprooted the
idea of subservience between human beings, as it desired to
give each individual his due honor and dignity. However,
the only instance in which subservience becomes acceptable
is when it is in the way of God. In those cases, subservience
renders the highest level of honor because a person is sub-

---

[6] The Holy Quran. Chapter 6. [The Cattle; Arabic: *Al-An'aam*]. Verse 151.
[7] The Holy Quran. Chapter 17. [The Night Journey; Arabic: *Al-Israa*]. Verse 23-
24.

mitting himself to his Lord and detaching from anything else.

God instructs us to submit to our parents with humility in the following verse. "And, out of kindness, lower to them the wing of humility, and say: 'My Lord, have mercy on them both as they did care for me when I was little.'"[8] Imam Al-Sadiq expanded on this verse when he said,

> Do not fill your eyes when you are looking at them except with mercy and compassion, and do not raise your voice over them... [Do not raise] your hand over their hands and do not walk ahead of them.[9]

Consequently, the relationship with the parents should be driven by humility, subservience, and mercy. This applies in all notwithstanding whether the parents are Muslims or not, pious or not. The Holy Quran makes this clear in the following verse,

> And if they contend with you that you should associate with Me what you have no knowledge of, do not obey them, and keep company with them in this world kindly, and follow the way of him who turns to Me, then to Me is your return, then will I inform you of what you did.[10]

Imam Al-Ridha said, "Doing good unto parents is obligatory, even if they are polytheists and they disobey God. However, there is no [obligation of] obedience to them in disobedience to the Creator."[11] Contrary to what some people

---

[8] The Holy Quran. Chapter 17. [The Night Journey; Arabic: *Al-Israa*]. Verse 23-24.

[9] Al-Reyshahri, *Mizan Al-Hikma*, 4:3677.

[10] The Holy Quran. Chapter 31. [Luqman; Arabic: Luqman]. Verse 15.

[11] Al-Reyshahri, *Mizan Al-Hikma*, 4:3677.

might believe, doing good towards our parents actually continues after their death as well. "And your parents, obey and
do good unto them alive or dead, and if they order you to
abandon your family [i.e. wife and children] and wealth, do
so because that is of faith,"[12] the Prophet directed. Imam
Al-Sadiq also said,

> What precludes man from doing good unto his parents alive
> or dead… praying, fasting, offering charity, and performing
> hajj on their behalf such that [the rewards of these acts] is
> for them and he will receive equal to that [reward] from
> God. God will increase his rewards for his good work and
> prayers with a great bounty."[13]

Guardianship and Obedience

One of the important matters in the relationship with the
parents is identifying the limitations to obedience. In that
respect, there are a number of specific religious laws that we
need to pay attention to.

First, there is the father's legal guardianship over his minors.
It is impermissible for minors to engage in any work without the father's permission. Every contract entered into by a
minor is considered void without the father's approval. This
guardianship continues until the minor reaches the age of
religious maturity[14].

---

[12] Ibid.

[13] Ibid.

[14] Religious maturity, or Buloogh, for a male is when he hits puberty or reaches
the age of 15; and for a female is when she reaches the age of 9. At this time, the
individual is required to observe obligations and responsibilities and is accountable for their actions. – Eds.

Second, although the guardianship terminates upon the son or daughter reaching the age of religious maturity, the children still have a continuous obligation to obey their parents. The parental orders that need to be obeyed by children irrespective of their age are referred to as 'Al-Awamir Al-Ishfaqiya' – orders of compassion. For example, if the mother or father disallow their son from traveling, fearing for his safety or concerned for his wellbeing, it is impermissible for him to defy their decision.

Third, it is obligatory on the children to spend on their parents when they are distressed financially. Financial assistance is not one way in this relationship. It is not merely the burden of the parents to provide for their children. When the parents are in financial need, their children have an obligation to provide for them as well.

Fourth, it is equally important to be aware that grandparents have the same right as parents to be obeyed. Although the issue of guardianship is different in some aspects, the grandparents enjoy the same rights as the parents. It is impermissible to avoid doing good to them. Additionally, one needs to fulfill the same obligations towards them as the parents including exercising respect, obedience, and subservience.

Disobedience to Parents

One of the greater sins a person can commit is disobeying his parents – gravely wronging them or completely disconnecting from them. If we revisit the narrations of Ahlulbayt, we find alarming examples of disobedience to parents amongst people. It is possible that we inadvertently engage in many of these practices that constitute disobedience to our parents, which is ultimately disobedience to God.

Imam Al-Sadiq said, "The most minimal [form of] disobedience is [saying] 'ouf' [i.e. sighing in discontent]... and if God [saw] anything less than that, he would have prohibited it."[15]

On another occasion, Imam Al-Sadiq described the abhorrence of someone who merely looks at his parents in the wrong way. "Whoever looks at his parents with repugnance, and they have oppressed him, God will not answer any of his prayers."[16]

We sense that the relationship between the children and their parents has changed due to today's culture and way of life. Unfortunately, many children belittle their parents because they may not be educated or have the best profession. These individuals need to understand that whatever they achieve in this life, be it education, status, or wealth, is due to the blessings of their parents. Your parents are everything. The roots of the blessings we see are our parents. The Prophet said, "Whoever aggrieves his parents has disobeyed them."[17]

Like obedience continues after the demise of the parents, disobedience can similarly transpire after their passing, as the narrations indicate. Imam Al-Baqir said in this regard,

If a servant is obedient to his parents in their lifetime but when they die, he does not pay their debt or ask God for

[15] Ibid.
[16] Ibid.
[17] Al-Majlisi, *Bihar Al-Anwar*, 71:72.

their forgiveness, God will record him as a disobeyer. And if he was disobedient to them during their lifetime but when they died, he paid their debt and asked [God] for their forgiveness, God will record him as obedient.[18]

When we discuss the issue of obedience and disobedience, it is imperative to realize that the mother is of a higher status than the father, although the father has legal religious guardianship and she does not. Nonetheless, the sacred texts instructed us about the mother much more than the father. It is narrated that a person came to the Prophet and asked, "O Messenger of God, who should I do good unto?" The Prophet replied, "Your mother." The man said, "Then who?" The Prophet replied again, "Your mother." Once more the man asked, "Then who?" The Prophet replied for the third time, "Your mother" The man then asked for a final time, "Then who?" The Prophet said, "Your father."[19]

The Effects in this Life and the Hereafter

Doing good unto parents and disobedience have ramifications that a person will witness in this life, as well as in the hereafter. The effects of doing good unto parents are a continuous pouring of blessings and mercy. The Prophet said, "Whoever would be happy if his life is prolonged, and his sustenance is increased, should do good to his parents and connect with his kinfolks."[20] Imam Al-Sadiq provides a wholistic perspective in addition to this when he said, "Do

---

[18] Al-Reyshahri, *Mizan Al-Hikma*, 4:3675.
[19] Ibid.
[20] Ibid.

good unto your parents, your children will do good to you."[21]

On the other hand, the effects of disobedience are devastating. Imam Al-Sadiq says, "Disobedience of parents is a major sin because God made the disobeyer a wretched sinner."[22] Imam Al-Hadi reaffirms this when he said, "Disobedience of parents will render poverty and result in disgrace."[23]

THE PARENTS' OBLIGATIONS

In the previous chapter, Raising a Child, we discussed a number of important obligations that parents owe to their children related to their nurturing and education. In that regard, it is important for parents to remember that when God blesses them with children, it does not mean that they are empowered to treat their children as slaves or peasants.

Children are a divine bounty that one needs to be grateful for. Furthermore, having a child is a massive responsibility that parents need to take seriously. Parents have the obligation to raise their children in a way that will help them succeed and prosper in this life and in the hereafter. The parents assume the responsibility to monitor their child's manners and behaviors so they can guide him through.

Thus, God granted children rights through the Holy Quran and the noble traditions. The following are only two of the many rights that children have. The first right is to be

---

[21] Ibid.

[22] Al-Reyshahri, *Mizan Al-Hikma*, 4:3677.

[23] Ibid.

taught, nurtured, and disciplined in a proper manner. The Prophet said, "The right of a child upon his father is for [the father] to teach him writing, swimming, archery, and to give him only what is good."[24] Imam Al-Sadiq also said, "A child is entitled to three things from his father: the selection of his mother, selection of a pleasant name, and discipline."[25]

Proper discipline and education cannot be achieved through violence or disparagement. Mercy cannot permeate in a society if a person does not see that mercy in the home he grows up in. We cannot expect a person to excel in his creativity and climb up the ladder of excellence if he lives in a state of fear at home. A father who makes his children live in constant terror and fear brings no value to his home and family.

The second right is for the father to do good unto his children. There are numerous narrations that stress this matter. In fact, these narrations state that the children doing good unto their parents is contingent on how the parents treat their children. If the parents do good towards their children, the children will reciprocate that. The Prophet alludes to this notion in a narration where he said, "May God have mercy on [a parent] who aids his children in doing good unto him – which is to forgive his shortcomings and to pray for him [i.e. child] between him and God."[26]

There are narrations that show the direct correlation between doing good to one's children and doing good to one's

24 Al-Hindi, *Kanz Al-'Ummal*, 16:443.

25 Al-Majlisi, *Bihar Al-Anwar*, 75:236.

26 Al-Kulayni, *Al-Kafi*, 6:50.

own parents. Imam Al-Sadiq said, "A man doing good unto his child is doing good unto his [own] parents."[27] In another tradition, a man asked Imam Al-Sadiq, "Who should I do good unto?" The Imam answered, "Your parents." The man replied, "[But] they passed away…" The Imam then said, "[Then] do good unto your children."[28]

Moreover, the narrations from the Prophet and his disciples address a pertinent issue relating to parents' violation of children's rights. The narrations specify that the ramifications of disobedience to one's parents similarly apply when the parents are the ones that commit injustice towards their own children. Parents must take care of their children and treat them with affection and compassion.

Parenting is an enormous task because through it individuals are developed and a community is built. It is not a minor undertaking. People who have wish to have many children because they like the idea of it need to be mindful. Quantity becomes meaningless if the children are not raised properly, giving them the needed time, education, nurturement, and discipline. Parents also have to regard their children's psychological state and make sure they build it by first leading by example with their own manners and actions. Imam Ali Al-Sajjad captures the right of a child in his renowned Treatise on Rights. He writes,

> *The right of your child is that you should know that he is from you and will be ascribed to you, through both his good and his evil, in the immediate affairs of this world. You are responsible for what has been entrusted to you, such as edu-*

---

[27] Al-Sadouq, *Man La Yahdaruh Al-Faqih*, 3:483.
[28] Al-Kulayni, *Al-Kafi*, 6:49.

cating him in good conduct, pointing him in the direction of his Lord, and helping him to obey Him. So act toward him with the action of one who knows that he will be rewarded for good doing toward him and punished for evildoing.[29]

---

[29] Al-Sadouq, *Man La Yahdaruh Al-Faqih*, 2:622.

FATHERS

And God has given you wives of your own kind, and has given you, from your wives, sons and grandsons, and has made provision of good things for you. Is it then in vanity that they believe and in the grace of God that they disbelieve?[1]

God created man, inspired him, and gave him what he needed to thrive in this world. With his God-given framework he is able to attain success in this life and next. This divinely constructed framework will ensure that man receives his rights and knows of his obligations, which will render balance, respect, and happiness for him and his community.

An essential part of this framework is the family unit. Like all other institutions, God has decreed a specific set of laws and rules that govern the functionality and management of the family. Each family member has a role to play that is vital for the success of the family and a wholesome environment that contributes to its growth. Parents hold the lion's

---

[1] The Holy Quran. Chapter 16. [The Bee; Arabic: *Al-Nahl*]. Verse 72.

share of responsibility in this regard. Fathers, in particular, are responsible for the wellbeing of the family and are tasked as guardians and wardens of the household. Before delving into the role of the father, it is important to discuss a few key issues.

The Makeup of Society

It is an amazing thing when something is constructed of multiple diverse components. It allows for versatility and flexibility in functionality. From computers and gadgets to organizations and institutions, diversity and multiplicity are usually apparent and key. This applies to human beings as well. Man is powerful with the versatility he has to function and manage his affairs. He observes with his eyes, smells with his nose, hears with his ears, and feels with his touch. We find that each of these parts plays a significant role and has its own impact.

This importance magnifies when all these parts come together and function in harmony. However, when the parts are separated and isolated, functionality can be compromised. Take a car for example. The engine, the frame, the headlights, the seats, the steering wheel, and the rest of the parts play a role in making the car work. When these parts are together they form a car that drives and takes us where we need to go. However, when you deconstruct the car into these individual parts, they become less useful or sometimes entirely useless. Moreover, to maintain the functionality of the car, you need all parts to be sound and functional. If any part is dysfunctional, it will detriment the overall functionality of the car. Society is the same way. Our parts make up the whole and each part is necessary for the whole to work the way it should. The family unit is perhaps one of the most, if not the most, important part of our society.

The Family: The Most Important Social Unit

The family is made up of a group of individuals. The health and wellbeing of each individual contributes to the overall health and functionality of the family. When more families are healthy and functioning, society will be healthier and more stable. The health of the family is often dependent on the strength of the bond and the affection shown amongst its members. It also relies on understanding and appreciating the rights and obligations of each family member. That will usher a family that is cognizant, productive, and respectful which in turn will produce a good and strong society.

Man is distinguished from other creatures because he is responsible and accountable for all of his actions. This put him in a special position relative to all other creatures. The Holy Quran addresses the issue of judgement in the Hereafter in a host of verses. God states, "And stop them, for they must be questioned."[2] In another verse, He speaks about the depth and extent of judgement on the Day of Resurrection,

> And We set a just balance for the Day of Resurrection so that no soul is wronged in aught. Though it be of the weight of a grain of mustard seed, We bring it. And We suffice for reckoners.[3]

---

[2] The Holy Quran. Chapter 37. [Those Drawn Up in Ranks: Arabic: *Al-Saaffaat*]. Verse 24.

[3] The Holy Quran. Chapter 21. [The Prophets: Arabic: *Al-Anbiyaa*]. Verse 47.

Judgement is increased and reduced depending on a person's intellectual maturity and ability. No doubt, as a person's status and position in society becomes more important, his accountability and responsibility will be greater. Furthermore, as his intellectual capacity grows and develops, his responsibility increases and his judgement will be with a higher standard of scrutiny.

It is narrated that Imam Al-Baqir said, "Servants will be scrutinized on the Day of Judgement based on their intellectual capacity in this world."[4] Thus, because the family is the most important social unit, it is valuable to discuss how to manage its affairs and who is responsible for that. It is equally important to discuss some of the negative practices related to the family and children in our communities.

THE FATHER'S ROLE IN THE HOUSEHOLD

God provided detailed guidelines regarding the management of the household. He specified the rights and obligations involved. Our focus here is on the role of the father and the extent of responsibility he has, particularly the matter of guardianship for his wife and children. The father is the keeper of his family because it is he who started the family. He is responsible for his marriage and the children that come from the marriage. It is his choice to start and grow the family, and thus his responsibility to maintain and protect it.

It is a part of the nature of man to seek immortality. Rationally, that is not possible and he realizes this. Thus, he

---

[4] Al-Kulayni, Al-Kafi, 1:9.

chooses to live vicariously through his offspring. Children are an essential part of one's own existence because they are his natural successorship. A man works to establish his family through marriage and having children. At that point, the man's responsibility and duty commences to take care and provide for his family. He is obliged to raise and nurture them properly and to ensure they are physically and spiritually healthy. In turn, the father becomes liable for any shortcomings in any of these areas. Contrary to what some may think, the mother is religiously not responsible or obliged to manage the affairs of the family. It is the responsibility of the father.

GUIDELINES FOR PROPER UPBRINGING

Assuming Responsibility

Some fathers do not feel a sense of duty towards their wives and children. They ignorantly assume that as the "head" of the family, the wife and children must serve them instead of the other way around. Some men feel a sense of entitlement in the home because they are the ones that provide for the family. No one will dispute that the father is responsible for providing for the family. However, that does not alleviate him from his other important responsibilities. Equally valuable, the father is responsible for his children's education and wellbeing. While it is true that Islam does grant the father specific rights such as the right to be respected and the right of religious guardianship, it is also true that his obligations are greater and he must be mindful of that.

Caring for the Hereafter

Deep immersion in worldly life and being occupied by the endless needs of this life might cause one to become heedless about his obligations affecting the hereafter. Life's hardships can especially take a toll on a father. He can easily become consumed with the immediate matters affecting his family. He thinks about their wellbeing and how the will succeed in life. His priorities are to enroll his children in good schools, encourage them to get in extracurricular activities for their physical and social health, and all in help provide them with the best of opportunities so they can live a comfortable life. Some may view the obligation of the father as strictly financial, or that at least financial sustainability is the most important obligation. The measure for success becomes one's ability to help his children land the best jobs and make the most income.

Although being concerned with providing a comfortable life for the family is positive and necessary, it is not everything. All of these worldly matters pave the way and prepare someone to become financially successful, but that does not necessarily translate into eternal prosperity. What is more important is that a person strikes the proper balance to secure one's livelihood while preparing for the eternal life in the hereafter. What good is it if he lives a prosperous life in this world but loses the hereafter?

Balance is key. As Imam Ali advised, we are to work for this life as if we live forever but work for the next life as if we die tomorrow. To achieve that balance, it is imperative to employ reason and intellect to prioritize successfully. Life, work, and comfort are all important. However, they cannot be at the cost of what lies ahead in our afterlife. It is essential that we raise our children with that balanced outlook. To strive and work hard in this life but never leave the afterlife out of their sight. That is the final destination and the everlasting goal. Our time in this life is but a number of years, but the afterlife is everlasting. The father assumes a great role in raising his children with this mindset. He must first himself have the maturity and understanding of this balance, so that he can impart its wisdom on his children. When the children see their father living based on this principle, they will likely follow.

Within a Community

As fathers, we need to keep the bigger picture of raising our children in mind. These kids will contribute to society one day. They can be its movers and shakers, or they can be part of its problem. As we raise our children we have to remind ourselves that they are the future of society. They will one day be fathers as well. The way we model and teach our children will affect the way they do so for their own. Even more immediately, the manner in which fathers raise their sons and daughters has a direct impact on the neighborhood they live in, the community they are a part of, and the society at large.

A well-mannered young woman is a source of pride and comfort for her neighbors and community. She is there when others need help and thinks about others before she thinks about herself. People will attribute her good manners to her upbringing and praise her parents. On the flip side, a not so well-mannered young man can be a cause of discomfort or trouble in a neighborhood and community. Similarly, his lack of manners will be attributed to his lack of upbringing. The parents are responsible for that. The child is their product – a reflection of their own.

Continuous Charity

Parents should realize that the process of upbringing is not limited in duration because the implications of raising children transcends generations. If a parent raises righteous children, he will have a positive continuity in this life. His deeds will not be terminated because he will be the source for his children and grandchildren's good deeds. From this understanding, we find that God has emphasized man's continuity after demise, as is narrated by Ishaq Ibn Ammar on the behalf of Imam Al-Sadiq,

> *Nothing will follow man after death except three things: a charity he offered for God that will continue for him after his death, a tradition of guidance he established which will be followed after his death, and a righteous son that supplicates for him.*[5]

A person's life does not terminate with his demise. His presence can continue through his children. A child can become an extension for his parent through his righteous deeds and supplications for them. The parent will garner rewards and blessings for his child's righteous acts. Keeping this framework in mind, the outlook for upbringing takes on a different level because the consequences become even more personal. When we realize that our children's actions in this life implicate our eternal destiny, we become even more invested in their upbringing. The tools and means of

---

[5] Al-Kulayni, Al-Kafi, 7:56.

raising our children are that much more important to ensure that the way we raise them is proper and better in quality.

NEGATIVE PRACTICES IN UPBRINGING

A moment of pause can do wonders for us, especially as fathers. It is key to take pause and reflect on what are we actually doing to raise our children. Due to a lack of attention or passivity, a person might not view, feel, or realize that certain upbringing practices are detrimental. Thus, it is imperative to highlight some of these negative practices and alert ourselves of them.

Being Occupied and Not Spending Time with Children

With today's fast pace lifestyle, we may find ourselves too occupied with the tasks of work and social life that we become distant from family. Working long days and possibly even nights, it can be easy to lose track of time and forget to spend the necessary time with our children. As fathers, we need to pay special attention to this because of the grave impact it can have over the long-term.

Though work is important, it is also important to realize the following. A person that consumes all of his time just working is defining his responsibility to his children as primarily financial. As we discussed previously, money is vital but it is not everything in life. A father is not only a financial provider because the family needs much more from the father than money. A family might be willing to live a modest life in exchange for a stronger and more effective presence of the father in the household. Most families cherish, and need, the presence of the father in the home to engage with the children and be there for them much more than living a lavish life.

A father is needed by the wife and children. As the guardian of the household, he must be present to serve and protect. Paying the bills is not enough. There are numerous life lessons and sorts of education that are uniquely imparted by a father, be it to a son or a daughter. A father's experience, knowledge, and strong demeanor are indispensable in the home. Children feed off of their father's presence and character. His presence and engagement with them boosts their confidence and builds their self-esteem.

Being occupied with providing sustenance probably has its justifications. However, it does not alleviate the father of his other duties. A father should fulfill all of his duties by allotting each one the adequate time and effort. A father must proactively allocate time, even if minimally, for his children. He needs to make them feel he truly cares for them and is there for them as their shoulder to lean on and that unwavering rock that has their back.

Relying on the Mother to Manage the Affairs of the Household

One of the negative practices that is prevalent in our communities is the father relying on his wife to manage the affairs of the household. He leaves the responsibility to her to raise the children and attend to their various needs. Though there is no doubt the mother holds her own in fundamentally raising her children, putting the burden solely on her is ill-advised. Children are in need of both the mother and father. The father's role cannot be assumed by the mother and vice versa. A mother can fulfill some of the vital functions in the home and attend to the major needs of the children, in addition to being their indispensable source of love and compassion. The mother's role is critical, but it needs to be complemented by the father.

The father plays an instrumental role in the children, especially with the boys. Young men go through a difficult period during puberty where they face colossal challenges. During that trying stage and beyond, young men need their father's support and guidance. The father is better positioned and equipped than the mother to help during this process. Beyond that, the father plays a vital role in monitoring his children, helping them resolve their social challenges, and keeping an eye on their outings and friends.

It is not possible for the mother to assume the role of the father and take on his load. It is already too challenging for the mother to fulfill her own role. In fact, she might need support and help herself, not to have another mountain of obligations thrown at her. It is unfair, ineffective, and a recipe for failure.

Failure in Prioritizing

This is another major issue. After work, some men make it a priority to spend their free time with their friends hanging out at late night gatherings and other outings. They justify it as a means to unwind after a long consuming day at work. It is a way to recover and recharge to prep for another busy day. Although it is important for a person to enjoy quality time with friends, it cannot be at the expense of family. The temporary leisure a person enjoys by spending time with friends will turn to misery and hardship if the children are essentially receiving the short end of the stick. Our faith instructs us to live life with moderation and balance. We should not adopt either extreme. Working eight or ten hours a day does not justify a person to spend another eight hours with friends to unwind, while leaving his wife and children behind at home. This is pure neglect that has detrimental consequences on the whole family.

Lack of Attention to the Religious Education

The most important obligation on the father is to teach his children their religion. Children should learn and embrace their faith. Unfortunately, some fathers do not give this aspect much importance. Fathers need to immerse their children in the religious and spiritual environments at a very young age. They should take their children with them to the mosque and majalis[6]. This will instill in the children a sense of love and affinity to the faith and its practices. Furthermore, by taking children and encouraging them to be in these positive religious environments, the children will develop an attachment and belonging to the mosque and other religious establishments. We find that this has been fading away in our communities. Some fathers are not willing to spend the time and effort to have their children accompany them to the mosque because they see it as merely an annoyance. We have to have patience with our children and realize that it takes time and attention to teach them what is right and wrong. Anything of quality needs quality time. We need to remember that as fathers who want to see their sons and daughters as true sources of pride and honor for them, in this life and the next.

---

[6] Gatherings of commemoration usually held at Islamic centers, held in memory of members of the Prophet's holy household. – Eds.

RELATIVES

In the name of God, the most Beneficent, the most Merciful

Is he then who knows that what has been revealed to you from your Lord is the truth like him who is blind? Only those possessed of understanding will mind, those who fulfil the promise of God and do not break the covenant, and those who join that which God has bidden to be joined and have awe of their Lord and fear the evil reckoning.[1]

As mothers and fathers, sons and daughters, we have to realize the great importance that lies in maintaining our ties with our families. One of the greatest relationships that God instructed us to embrace is our kinship. Our kin is defined as anyone that the social custom defines as a relative, ranging from grandparents, parents, and siblings to aunts, uncles, and cousins.

Building and maintaining relations with our relatives is a religious and ethical obligation. It becomes even more significant today because the notion of maintaining relations is fading slowly but surely. Remaining close to family members and embracing our heritage is becoming something of

---

[1] The Holy Quran. Chapter 13. [The Thunder; Arabic: *Al-Ra'ad*]. Verse 19-21.

the past. While our grandparents and parents made sure to maintain these connections, it is not something we find in our lives today. Unfortunately, we find that due to contemporary culture and shift in focus from the large communal family to the nuclear family, and now a type of modern family, the growing trend is that people are generally less concerned with staying connected to their kin. If this trajectory continues, we will soon be departing from any semblance of a family and be concerned merely with ourselves.

The shift in society, moving from being family centric to individualistic has serious ramifications. When we briefly observe communities that have abandoned family relations and embraced pure individualism, we find natural deterioration in family relationships. Family relations have become motivated by interest. A son merely sees his father as a way to advance his goals. He will embrace his father as long as he is benefitting and will abandon him otherwise. A husband views his wife as an instrument for entertainment, feeding his sexual hunger. When she no longer is able to serve this purpose, she will be neglected and left behind. Self-centered relationships never serve a true long-lasting purpose.

Islam's View on Connecting with Family

Islam advocates for social cohesion and communication between individuals. This call is not merely to promote the exchange of dialogue between people. Instead, the Islamic framework for building a community rests on creating a righteous collective, not just a righteous individual. Islam does not promote individualistic worship. In fact, we find a strong community element in worship acts and rituals. A righteous community creates a righteous individual, but the inverse is not always true. A righteous individual might not be able to impact and change the status of his or her corrupt community. Therefore, Islam has rejected monastic life.

We find that the first social institution that Islam sought to protect is the family. A person is fully responsible for his or her family members. Imam Ali describes this in his eloquent words, "All of you are shepherds, and you are all responsible for your herds."[2]

Accordingly, this social institution expands to include the greater family, clan and tribe. Every institution connects its members to enhance their social bond because that will inevitably reflect on the greater community.

Caring for family has a tremendous impact in preserving person's journey in this life. They are his wings allowing him to fly and ascend to the highest levels of success and fortune. They are his hands which he strikes with to shatter all obstacles impeding his way. When a person becomes concerned about the community as a whole, he will be more invested in the collective than just the individual. This mindset will help propel the community forward. That is why we find that in certain cases while applying Islamic jurisprudence, a person's wrongdoings implicate not only himself but also his blood relatives. It becomes a collective responsibility on the family to mitigate the situation.

Considering all of this, Islam puts special emphasis on building and maintaining relations with blood relatives. This conduct becomes more than just a social phenomenon it is

---

[2] Al-Ahsae'i, 'Awali Al-La'ali, 1:129.

a form of obedience that pleases God. Consequently, severing family ties is considered a callous act that is rejected by God and is a departure from His obedience.

Strengthening the Spirit of Belonging

God has placed a special emphasis on a person's sense of belonging. As human beings we cannot rid ourselves of others and live in isolation. Even if we do, such a state is usually accompanied by misery and loneliness, which we naturally dread. We yearn for companionship and getting to know others. This is how we were created, it is how we are wired. God states in the Holy Quran,

> *O you men! Surely We have created you of a male and a female, and made you tribes and families that you may know each other; surely the most honorable of you with God is the most righteous of you.*[3]

Within the social fabric, there are units that a person feels a need to belong to, such as a tribe (extended family) or a nation. The most important social units are the family and tribe. If the attachment is weak, this will affect the state of belonging to all other social units. Our attachment and engagement to others is part of our humanity. Our care, concern, and compassion for one another is what makes us human. If a person cannot engage with others and deal with them through compassion and mercy, he has lost the most essential part of his humanity. There is a reference to this in the Holy Quran where God states, "...they are like cattle,

---

[3] The Holy Quran. Chapter 49. [The Inner Apartments; Arabic: *Al-Hujraat*]. Verse 13.

nay, they are more misguided… these are the heedless ones."[4]

God stresses on belonging and being part of a collective as opposed to isolation and seclusion. A sense of belonging renders strength and honor. Imam Ali puts this in perspective for us where he says,

> *O people, surely a man cannot dispense of his kin even if he were wealthy, he needs their protection of him by their hands and their tongues. They have the most precaution with respect to him, the most caring for his affairs, the most compassionate when ill strikes him. Surely, an honest tongue of praise that God would create for a man amongst others is better than wealth which he will impart to others as an inheritance.[5]*

Imam Ali continues in the same sermon,

> *Behold! If any one of you finds your near ones in want or starvation, he should not desist from helping them with that which will not increase if this help is not extended, nor decrease by thus spending it. Whoever prevents his hand from helping his kinsmen, he prevents one hand, but at the time of his need many hands remain prevented from helping him. One who is sweet tempered can retain the love of his people for good.[6]*

Strengthening Community Through the Cohesion of Small Units

Islam has always preached for building a strong cohesive community. Islam views community building as a desirable

---

[4] The Holy Quran. Chapter 7. [The Heights; Arabic: *Al-A'araaf*]. Verse 179.
[5] Al-Radhi, *Nahj Al-Balagha*, Sermon 23.
[6] Ibid.

goal that ought to be supported. There is no doubt that building small units on a strong foundation will result in a durable enduring community. A stronger bond between these small units and more shared commonalities will of course render greater cohesion. A person is connected to his kin with more shared commonalities than he is with other groups of people, such as neighbors, friends, colleagues, or others. Greater commonalties will foster stronger bonds. Thus, connecting with kin naturally leads to strength in that community.

We find that Lady Zahra states in one of her sermon's, "God has ordained for connecting with kinship to be a multiplier for numbers."[7] Large numbers is a source of strength and connecting with kinship will render this effect. This phenomenon could have a natural explanation as good relations and connectivity between relatives, might result in a greater likelihood to have marriages which will render more offspring and good pious individuals. There are other narrations that describe other signs of strength rendered through good relations with family.

The Holy Prophet said, "Fear God and have good relations with your relatives, for that is better for you in this life and a blessing for you in the hereafter."[8] There is another narration by the Prophet which is even more explicit in explaining the impact of good relations with kin on strengthening the community. He said, "Good relations with familial relations builds homes and prolongs lives, even if its people [i.e.

---

[7] Al-Majlisi, *Bihar Al-Anwar*, 71:94.

[8] Al-Hindi, *Kanz Al-'Ummal*, 3:356.

the ones pursuing good relations with their kinfolks] are not righteous."[9]

Strengthening the Spirit of Solidarity

Islam is a religion of social solidarity and community support. One that promotes charity for the sake of God and considers offering financial help to the needy as a loan to God truly has a great return.

> *Who is it that will lend unto God a righteous loan, so He will multiply return it to him manifold, and God straightens and amplifies, and you shall be returned to Him.*[10]

There are dozens of verses that call on us to offer in the way of God, by supporting the less fortunate and fulfilling their needs. Spending one's own money is not an easy task. Most problems that people have and many of the sins they commit is rooted in money. Offering charity is something that we must train ourselves to do, so that it becomes a normal part of our conduct and behavior.

Our families, of course, are the first and foremost when it comes to our giving. The reasons for offering charity in this sort are numerous. There is a strong bond involved – blood and family. Many of the blessed verses mention charity and its benefits. Because of the importance family ties, helping and supporting them is a priority. We have a greater responsibility to extend a helping hand to family before anyone else.

If our own families need our help and we do not come to their aid, what does that say about us? We should not look

---

[9] Al-Majlisi, *Bihar Al-Anwar*, 71:94.
[10] The Holy Quran. Chapter 2. [The Cow; Arabic: *Al-Baqara*]. Verse 245.

too far; instead, we should start with them. When every person fulfills his obligations by helping those in need, starting with those closest to us, poverty will diminish in our communities. "Reaching out to kinfolks improves manners, increases generosity, cures the soul, boosts sustenance, and delays death,"[11] said Imam Al-Sadiq.

RELIGIOUS RULINGS RELATED TO RELATIVES

There are a host of religious rulings pertaining to kinfolks generally and others specific to particular family members.

Obligation to Maintain Relations with Relatives

Maintaining relations with family members is not just recommended, it is religiously obligatory. The application of this obligation comes in various ways. It includes visiting those family members, checking up on them, supporting them financially, fulfilling their needs, and at a bare minimum, sending greetings and praying for them. The objective should be to avoid disconnecting or severing one's relationship with them. The closer the family member is to you, the more rights he has on you as is illustrated by Imam Ali Ibn Al-Husayn in *The Treatise on Rights*,

> *The rights of womb relatives are many, it is connected to the proximity of the relationship of the blood relative. The greatest obligation is the right of your mother, then the right of your father, then [the right] of your children, then [the right] of your sibling, then [the right] of those closest to you [in order based on the proximity of the relationship].*[12]

---

11 Al-Kulayni, Al-Kafi, 2:151.
12 Al-Harrani, *Tohaf Al-'Oqool*, 256.

The Impermissibility of Severing Relations with Kinfolks

Our jurists have mentioned that one of the major sins, sins which result in hellfire, is severing relations with family members - where a person abandons doing any good to his blood relatives. The Holy Quran is explicit in highlighting the severity of this act. It is mentioned subsequent to the act of spreading corruption in this world in the verse, "But if you held command, you were sure to make mischief in the land and cut off the ties of kinship."[13]

There are numerous traditions about this issue that alarm people of the severe consequences of cutting ties with blood relatives. The Prophet said, "Three will not enter paradise; an alcohol addict, a witchcraft addict, and one who severs relations with womb relatives."[14] Hathifa Ibn Mansour narrates a conversation he had with Imam Al-Sadiq. "Abu Abdullah said, 'Fear that which severs, for it kills men.' I said, 'What is that which severs?' He said, 'Severing ties with womb relatives.'"[15]

The obligation to embrace family ties and not sever relationships with those of kin does not only encompass Muslims. On the contrary, it extends to non-Muslims, enemies, and individuals themselves that have severed family ties, as is mentioned in the narrations. As to fostering relationships with non-Muslim relatives, Safwan narrates from Al-Jaham Ibn Hameed,

---

[13] The Holy Quran. Chapter 47. [Muhammad; Arabic: *Muhammad*]. Verse 22.
[14] Al-Sadouq, *Al-Khisal*, 179.
[15] Al-Kulayni, *Al-Kafi*, 2:346.

I told Abu Abdullah that I have a family member that follows a different way [i.e. non-Muslim], does he have a right on me? He said, 'Yes, nothing terminates the right of blood relatives. If they follow your [Islamic] path, they have two rights, the right of blood relatives and right of Islam. [16]

With regards to the importance of maintaining relations even with those that have cut ties Imam Al-Sadiq stated, "The Messenger of God said, 'Do not cut ties with blood relatives even if they have cut ties with you.'"[17]

Another narration illustrates a conversation between the Holy Prophet and a man who was concerned with severing ties with some of his family members. He told the Prophet, "O Messenger of God, I have relatives that I used to maintain relations with... when they used to harm me I wanted to reject them..." The Prophet replied to him, "Then God will reject all of you..." Concerned, the man then asked "So what should I do?" The Prophet answered, "Give to those who deprived you, connect with those who cut ties with you, and forgive those who oppressed you... if you do so, God will protect you from them."[18]

Financial Support for Relatives and Kinfolks

It is obligatory to provide financial support to some relatives such as parents. Further, it is an obligatory precaution to support maternal and paternal grandparents as well as children, grandchildren, and any descending issue.

---

[16] Al-Majlisi, *Bihar Al-Anwar*, 71:131.

[17] Al-Kulayni, *Al-Kafi*, 2:347.

[18] Al-Majlisi, *Bihar Al-Anwar*, 71:100.

As to other blood relatives, it is not obligatory to spend on them although it is in fact recommended. Looking into the history of the Prophet's progeny, you will see that they even maintained relations with hostile relatives that routinely attacked them. It is narrated by Salma, one of Imam Al-Sadiq's servants, that the Imam connected with womb relatives who in turn severed ties with him. Salma said,

> I was with Abu Abdullah Ja'far Ibn Muhammad when death approached him and he went into unconsciousness. When he woke up he said, 'Grant Al-Hassan Ibn Ali Ibn Al-Husayn seventy Dinars and give this person this amount and this person that amount...' I said, 'Do you give to a man who held a blade desiring to kill you?' The [Imam] replied, 'Do you not want me to be amongst those that God describes in the Holy Quran, And those who join that which God has bidden to be joined and have awe of their Lord and fear the evil reckoning[19]... Yes, Salma, God created paradise and has beautified it and beautified its fragrance... its fragrance can be smelled from a distance of two thousand years, [however] the one who disobeys his parents or severs relations with his womb relatives will not smell it.[20]

Inheritance

One of the issues that is related to blood relatives is inheritance. God has decreed for inheritance to be distributed to three hierarchal levels of relatives. If the first level of heirs is present, the second level is precluded, and if the second is present, the third is precluded. The first level of heirs in-

---

[19] The Holy Quran. Chapter 13. [The Thunder; Arabic: *Al-Ra'd*]. Verse 21.
[20] Al-Kulayni, *Al-Kafi*, 7:55.

cludes the father, mother, children, and grandchildren. The second level includes maternal and paternal grandparents and any ascending issue, siblings, and children of siblings and any descending issue. The third and final level encompasses paternal and maternal uncles and any ascending issue, such as maternal and paternal great uncles, and their descending issue.

This is all detailed in our books of jurisprudence. Additionally, it is recommended to grant inheritance to blood relatives that are present during inheritance distributions even if they are not deserving heirs. This is illustrated in the Holy Quran, "And when kinsfolk and orphans and the needy are present at the division [of the inheritance], bestow on them therefrom and speak kindly unto them."[21]

Blood Money

There are religious rulings that implicate the tribe and family of a person in situations where there is an involuntary manslaughter and blood money needs to be paid. This further underscores the social support system in Islam. Islamic jurisprudence states that if a person unintentionally kills someone, he does not solely become responsible to pay the blood money. It becomes a collective responsibility on the culprit's tribe. The tribe is defined as all men that are related through the father such as brothers, uncles, and others. There are much more complex rulings regarding this matter that can be researched further and referenced in the books of jurisprudence.

---

[21] The Holy Quran. Chapter 4. [The Women; Arabic: *Al-Nisaa*]. Verse 8.

REASONS FOR SEVERING TIES WITH RELATIVES

Diagnosing the reasons for a problem will help in developing its solutions. We ask, what are the reasons that cause or contribute to severing family ties and the distancing between relatives? Perhaps if we answer this question, we can attempt to avoid falling into this great problem. There are a few primary factors that can contribute to the severing of family relations.

Contact Can Render Problems

It is very natural for a group of people with similar circumstances that are in constant contact with one another to have challenges and issues. These problems or disputes might crop up due to differences in preferences or habits between individuals. It can often be due to simple misunderstandings fueled by passion or emotion that is coming from another issue that one or both of the individuals is facing from a different context. The baggage from one experience pours into the engagement with others in another context. People feel disrespected or neglected and words are exchanged. Things escalate and people stop talking to each other. Other family members may get involved and the problem widens even further.

This is common series of events, and people can fill in the content that is unique to their situation. We need to be conscious of this matter and not allow for simple differences and minor problems to escalate to the point where relationships are severed and families break up. Our faith is not lenient when it comes to cutting family off. It is a big ordeal. If we cannot take care of our own families, through patience and compassion, how can we take care of the rest of our community?

The Social and Financial Disparity

Sadly, one of the things that contributes to blood relatives distancing themselves from one another – intentionally or inadvertently – is social and financial disparity. Money or power, or both, can have a tremendous effect on a man. It can be a source of pride and arrogance, both of which can drive a man away from the closest people to him. When man looks at himself as better than others, there is where his problems begin.

There is no problem with wealth or position in society. Many of God's prophets enjoyed both luxuries during their lifetimes. However, they used them as tools in the way of God. And they never looked down on anyone. For some, however, it is sadly not the case. The Holy Quran alludes to this, "Nay, man does transgress all bounds, in that he looks upon himself as self-sufficient."[22]

Being Occupied with Material and Worldly Matters

Unfortunately, people do not value social and family relations as they did in the past. People are busy and they justify their lack of family engagement with being occupied by their material affairs. This dynamic has resulted in people separating and being distant from one another.

Working for a livelihood is viewed as sacred by Islam. In fact, Islam advocates for people to work hard in their professions and strive provide for their families. However, Is-

---

[22] The Holy Quran. Chapter 96. [The Clot; Arabic: *Al-'Alaq*]. Verse 6-7.

lam objects when work transforms and becomes the 'lord that people worship' and where it becomes the end that occupies a person day and night. Our Imams teach us to live our lives with balance and moderation. Like we allocate time for our work, we need to allocate time for family. We need to make family members a priority by visiting them, checking up on them, and providing them with help when we can. This is an obligation that we cannot continue to ignore.

Intellectual Differences

Intellectual or ideological differences between members of the same family can also cause rifts. Islam does stand against expressing love and affection to the enemies of God, even if they are the closest of blood relatives. God illustrates that in the Holy Quran,

> *You shall not find a people who believe in God and the latter day befriending those who act in opposition to God and His Messenger, even though they were their [own] fathers, or their sons, or their brothers, or their kinsfolk.*[23]

Even then, Islam refuses the severing of relationships. The Holy Quran states, "And if they contend with you that you should associate with Me what you have no knowledge of, do not obey them, and keep company with them in this world kindly."[24]

Safwan narrates on the behalf of Al-Jaham Ibn Hameed, "I informed Abu Abdullah, 'I have relatives that do not follow

---

[23] The Holy Quran. Chapter 58. [The Pleading Woman; Arabic: *Al-Mujaadila*]. Verse 22.
[24] The Holy Quran. Chapter 31. [Luqman; Arabic: *Luqman*]. Verse 15.

my way; do they have a right over me?' He said, 'Yes, the right of womb relatives is not severed by anything.'"[25]

Based on that, we find that regardless severing relationships with family is not an option. If we are instructed to maintain relationships even with those that do not share our creed, what can we say about those that we might differ on with an opinion, thought, or idea? In these situations, there should be no disconnect in the relationship in any event. On the contrary, mercy and compassion should dictate our decisions in our relationships at all times.

It is disheartening to find people severing their family ties due to simple disagreements on opinions and preferences. We should not expect people to share our opinions or adopt our standards. Preferences are one thing and principles are another. And even when differing on principles, God still tells us not to cut off family.

THE EFFECTS: GOOD AND BAD

We have a host of noble narrations that speak about the effects of maintaining and severing relations with womb relatives in this life. One of the major positive effects of maintaining relations is increase in substance and prolonging of life.

The Prophet is narrated to have said, "Maintaining relations [with blood relatives] prolongs life and precludes poverty."[26] He adds in another tradition, "Whoever desires to have his

---

25 Al-Kulayni, *Al-Kafi*, 2:157.
26 Al-Majlisi, *Bihar Al-Anwar*, 71:88.

sustenance increased and his life prolonged, ought to maintain relations with blood relatives."[27]

Imam Al-Baqir said "We found in the Prophet's book, 'if they cut ties with their blood relatives, wealth will be in the hands of the wicked.'"[28] On another occasion Imam Al-Baqir described,

> *When a tribe is corrupt and they are not righteous, but they maintain relations with their kinfolk, their wealth will increase and their lives will prolong... [imagine] how it would be if they were righteous.*[29]

Another tangible positive impact of maintaining relations with kinfolks is that it will ease the pangs of death. Imam Al-Hadi describes that in a tradition,

> *In what Prophet Moses addressed God with, he said, 'O Lord what is the reward for maintaining ties with blood relatives?' God answered him, 'I will prolong his life and will ease the pangs of death on him.'*[30]

Addressing this matter, the Prophet said, "Maintaining relations with kinfolks eases judgement and prevents an ill death."[31]

Alternatively, as we have mentioned previously, severing ties with womb relatives has severe detrimental consequences. The Prophet addresses this issue in a striking narration where he states, "A person who severs relations with his

---

27 Ibid.
28 Ibid.
29 Al-Kulayni, *Al-Kafi*, 2:155.
30 Al-Sadouq, *Al-Amaali*, 276.
31 Al-Majlisi, *Bihar Al-Anwar*, 71:94.

kinfolks does not sit with us [i.e. Holy Household], for mercy does not descend on a tribe that has someone who severs family relations."[32]

Letting the words of the Holy Prophet and his disciples inspire us and guide our conduct and engagement with family is instrumental. We all have challenges and difficulties. We all face trial and tribulation. There are frustrations that make us want to do things we know we should not. Holding on to their inspiration will help us in our times of anger, confusion, and despair. God sent them to us for a reason. To guide us through, especially when we need it the most.

---

[32] Al-Kulayni, *Al-Kafi*, 2:348.

BIBLIOGRAPHY

RELIGIOUS SCRIPTURE

The Holy Quran

OTHER SOURCES

Al-Ahsa'i, Muhammad ibn Ali. *'Awali Al-La'ali*. Qum: Sayyid Al-Shuhada, 1983.

Al-Amili, Muhammad ibn Al-Hassan. *Wasa'el Al-Shia*. Beirut: Daar Ihya Al-Torath Al-Arabi.

Al-Barqi, Ahmad ibn Muhammad. *Al-Mahasin*. Tehran: Daar Al-Kutub Al-Islamiya, 1950.

Al-Hakeem, Muhammad Baqir. *Daur Ahlulbayt fi Bina al-Jama'a al-Saliha*. Qum: Al-Alami, 1997.

Al-Harrani, Al-Hassan ibn Ali. *Tohaf Al-'Oqool*. Qum: Muasasat Al-Nashr Al-Islami, 1983.

Al-Hindi, Ali Al-Muttaqi. *Kanz Al-'Ummal*. Muasasat Al-Risala, 1989.

Al-Khoei, Abulqasim. *Minhaj al-Saliheen*. Qum: Madinat al-'Ilm.

Al-Kulayni, Muhammad ibn Yaqoub. *Al-Kafi*. Tehran: Daar Al-Kutub Al-Islamiya, 1968.

Al-Majlisi, Muhammad Baqir. *'Ain Al-Hayat*. Qum: Muasasat Al-Nashr Al-Islami, 2000.

Al-Majlisi, Muhammad Baqir. *Bihar Al-Anwar*. Beirut: Al-Wafaa, 1983.

Al-Nouri, Mirza Hussain. *Mustadrak Al-Wasa'el*. Beirut: Mu'asasat Aal Al-Bayt li Ihya' Al-Torath.

Al-Qummi, Ali ibn Ibrahim. *Tafseer al-Qummi*. Qum: Dar al-Kitab, 1984.

Al-Radi, Muhammad ibn Al-Hussain. *Nahj Al-Balagha*. Beirut: Daar Al-Ma'rifa.

Al-Reyshahri, Muhammad. *Mizan Al-Hikma*. Cairo: Daar Al-Hadith, 1995.

Al-Sadouq, Muhammad ibn Ali. *'Oyun Akhbar Al-Rida*. Beirut: Al-A'lami, 1984.

Al-Sadouq, Muhammad ibn Ali. *Al-Amaali*. Qum: Muassasat Al-Bitha, 1996.

Al-Sadouq, Muhammad ibn Ali. *Al-Khisal*. Qum: Jama'at Al-Mudarriseen, 1983.

Al-Sadouq, Muhammad ibn Ali. *Man La Yahdaruh Al-Faqih*. 2nd ed. Qum: Jama'at Al-Mudarriseen.

Al-Sadouq, Muhammad ibn Ali. *Musadaqat al-Ikhwan*. Kadhimiya: Maktabat al-Imam Sahib al-Zaman, 1982.

Al-Siyouti, Abdulrahman. *Al-Dur Al-Manthur*. Beirut: Daar al-Ma'rifa.

Al-Tabrasi, Ahmad ibn Ali. *Al-Ihtijaj*. Najaf: Al-Nu'man, 1966.

Al-Tabrasi, Ameen Al-Deen. *Majama' Al-Bayan*. Beirut: Al-A'lami, 1995.

Al-Tabrasi, Radi Al-Deen. *Makarim Al-Akhlaq*. Manshurat Al-Shareef Al-Radi, 1972.

Al-Tousi, Muhammad ibn Al-Hassan. *Al-Amaali*. Qum, 1993.

Ibn Hanbal, Ahmad. *Musnad Ahmad*. Beirut: Daar Saadir.

Ibn Shahrashoob, Muhammad ibn Ali. *Al-Manaqib*. Najaf: Al-Matbaa Al-Haydaria, 1956.